Endorsements

Jules bares her soul in her beautifully written memoir 'Fool Me Twice' in an attempt to help others learn from her experiences. This is definitely a must-read for all the women out there.
– Joanne Ong, international bestselling author of 'The Sun Within: Rediscover You'

I first met Jules on one of the many podcasting enthusiasts' pages littered across social media. From the outset, I could tell that she was driven. We helped promote her small but growing podcast 'Hong Kong Confidential' on our network. The show about a woman from the country in South Australia talking to interesting people in Hong Kong steadily built an audience and hit new milestones. This is due in no small part to her work ethic and likeable personality. Jules's storytelling too has great depth; it can be funny but also dark in places. Her podcast is a unique offering. Get yourself a copy of the new book 'Fool Me Twice' by Jules Hannaford; you'll be glad you did.
– Liam Carter, Auscast Network

Jules's raw and honest personal account of her struggles is a beautiful example of how owning our own stories gives each of us the power to write a brave new ending.
– Rebecca Hopkins, Live Brave workshops

'Fool Me Twice' was written by Jules Hannaford about her life experiences with online dating. This story has many universal themes that will resonate with you, the reader. The purpose of the book is to educate others in the hope that no one will ever experience what she has: being scammed. Her advice is priceless and listening to her may save you from being scammed. A must-read for anyone considering internet dating.
– Judy O'Beirn, international bestselling author of the 'Unwavering Strength' series

A deep bow of respect to you, Jules, for seeking out and showing up to do the inner work we did together for you to reconnect with the creative, confident, vibrant parts of yourself that had been tucked away and forgotten about. You showed the curiosity, courage, love, and tenacity to do what you needed to give us your true, wondrous, radiant self!
– Natalie Goni, Life Coach

Jules, reading your awesome book was a treat even in the difficult, emotional parts. Having known you and your daughter for two decades on our little island paradise in Hong Kong, I was pleasantly surprised how much I enjoyed the book and learned so much from what you wrote. You're an inspiring mother, teacher, writer, artist, podcaster, person, firefighter, problem-solver, and most of all, friend to all of us. Keep up the great work, and thanks for everything.
– Glen Watson, Editor/Writer, Hong Kong

Internet dating scams are sadly an all-too-painful reality for many women in today's world, and most of us have no idea this is going on! It's hard to explain how intelligent, successful women with everything going for them can fall into this kind of trap, and yet they do. Every day.
If you ever wonder how is that possible, Jules's brave bare-it-all story of how she overcame the pain and shame of being involved in such a traumatic experience is an invaluable resource for women who may feel the need to go to great lengths to find real love.
After coaching many women in this situation to regain their self-esteem and trust that not all men are scammers and to overcome their pain and limiting beliefs related to love and relationships, I am delighted to see a true story of a woman who got her power back and is now ready to share her experience with the world.
Don't imagine this can never happen to you! Jules's practical tips on how to protect yourself and unmask these aggressors is a wonderful guide for every woman out there, so don't delay!
– Valentina Tudose, Dating and Relationship Coach, Happy Ever After

FOOL ME TWICE

GONFESSIONS OF A PERPETUAL INTERNET DATING NEOPHYTE

A MEMOIR
BY JULES HANNAFORD

Published by
Hasmark Publishing
www.hasmarkpublishing.com

Permission should be addressed in writing to Julie Hannaford at juliehannaford@hotmail.com

Editor: Online Author's Office
(www.thecappuccinochronicles.com)

Senior Editors: Zara Hannaford and Heather Floyd

Graphic Designer / Layout Artist: Rochelle Villaflores Sun

Layout Team: Anne Karklins and Online Author's Office
(pashmina.p.writer@gmail.com)

ISBN 13: 978-1-989161-32-6
ISBN 10: 1989161324

Dedication

To my beautiful, talented, and amazing daughter.
Thank you for your support and love.

Acknowledgements

I wish to say a huge thank you to everyone who supported me on my journey while writing this memoir. I am particularly grateful to the Online Author's Office, led by Pashmina P., for their endless encouragement and professionalism whilst bringing this book to fruition. To the editors, designers, researchers, and consultants from the OAO, I could not have done this without you. To Judy O'Beirn from Hasmark Publishing, thank you for selecting me as a client; I appreciate your faith in me. To all of my friends and family who have not only supported me through the process of writing my book but have also agreed to be in the book and allowed me to use their real names, I am very appreciative. Thank you also to those people who provided such heart-warming quotes about me to use in my book. Your generosity of spirit is truly amazing. Thank you so much to everyone who endorsed my book; your advocacy gives me strength. Your belief in me and your recognition that this is a story that needs to be told and understanding that it can help others is very humbling. I appreciate the support and guidance of the Principal of my school. Thanks to my daughter for your brilliant editing skills and wise advice. Thanks to Glen Watson for your editing support. Finally, special thanks to Mari, who has been with me on this journey every step of the way. Thanks for being my rock, my advisor, my mentor, and my dear friend.

Empathy is the antidote to shame.
—Brené Brown

Loving ourselves through the process of owning our story is the bravest thing we'll ever do.
—Brené Brown

Table of Contents

My Childhood

Aussie Farm Girl

My earliest memory is when I was three years old and my mum gave birth to twins at only six months along in her pregnancy. Days after they were born, my dad took me and my younger sister to hospital to see one of the babies who was being kept in a humidicrib. I have a very clear memory of walking down the corridor of the hospital with the silhouette of my dad and sister in front of me holding hands. The smell of disinfectant lingered around us, and an eerie, mottled light reflected off the shiny surface of the hospital floor. Our footsteps echoed in the long corridor, and it felt so peaceful as we walked in silence. I did not fully understand the gravity of the situation.

The boy, Ben, lived for only three days, and the girl, Sarah, survived for sixteen. When they died, the hospital rang my mum at home on the farm and said they were gone. She was never offered any support or counselling at all and just had to get on with it. Later, she ran into a doctor from a neighbouring town coming out of the local hardware store, and he stopped and said to her that given they were born so prematurely, if they had survived they may have had problems with their lungs or their development. This gave my mum a lot of comfort, but that was the only support a professional ever offered her. Her own doctor never mentioned the twins again. This is a sad indictment of Australia's medical system in the 1960s, but I suppose awareness about mental health issues and the benefits of counselling were not evident in that era.

I grew up on a farm in the mid north of South Australia with my little sister and, later, our little brother. I had a great upbringing in the country swimming, playing sport, and working on the farm. I did everything from hoeing thistles to fighting fires, but was quite a reluctant farm girl, despite being a tomboy. I preferred swimming and roller-skating around the town rather than working on the farm, as was expected of me. I babysat local children and had lots of friends in the small town of Riverton. I was a leader and very responsible at a young age, and as a teen, I was very sensible but had a wild streak lurking underneath just waiting to burst forth.

Our farm was 611 acres of land in prime farming country and has been in the family for six generations. Susanna Hannaford, a widow with eight sons, emigrated from the UK to Australia in the early 1800s and settled at Cudlee Creek. Her son John bought a farm at Riverton and initially owned a huge amount of land in the area that has since been sold off to three other families. Our old homestead, Wattle Vale, was managed by one of John and his wife Elizabeth's ten children, Alf Hannaford. Alf apparently went broke because he spent all his time trying to create inventions in the Blacksmith's Shop on the farm. It was a building made out of old railway sleepers with a dirt floor and a blacksmith's forge and anvil inside, along with many old tools from that era. Dad tried to preserve the old 'Blacksmith's Shop,' as we called it, for as long as he could by tying wire around it to hold it up, but eventually, the sleepers rotted away and it fell down. The family still has the old anvil and forge stored in a shed on the farm, and have offered it to the local museum. Alf Hannaford finally found success when he invented the Hannafords Seed Grader. It was used all over Australia and Africa, and Alf became a wealthy man from his invention. Meanwhile, Alf's brother, my great-grandfather Sam Hannaford, took over the farm, and that's how my family ended up living at Wattle Vale.

In the heart of the Gilbert Valley, Wattle Vale is situated at the base of a set of rolling hills and a small creek runs through it. The creek used to flow constantly fifty years ago, fed by a spring from up in the hills, but it has dried up and now only flows after a heavy rain. The land is a gently undulating mix of rich, earthy colours, which change drastically from season to season. In the winter, it is green and fertile, and in the summer, it is burnt orange and yellow, as the land gets incredibly dry. The temperature in the summer can reach the high 40s (Celsius), so hot that you can't touch the steering wheel or the metal seatbelt clasp when you get in your car. The farmhouse, built in 1869, is surrounded by gum trees planted by our great-grandmother, and we had free-range pigs roaming around in the paddock next to the house for many years. We grew lucerne, also known as alfalfa, to feed the pigs, and we used to cut the lucerne with an old-fashioned scythe. Wattle Vale is mainly a sheep farm, but we also grew crops of wheat, oats, and barley. It is a beautiful farm that has supported our family for generations. I was so lucky to grow up in such a wonderful place.

Mum and Dad met in the early 1960s when Mum moved to Riverton to teach in the local primary school. Mum was a beautiful young woman with a vibrant personality, and Dad was a handsome young man who played football and worked on the farm with his father. I always thought of Dad as a more handsome version of Jerry Lewis. Dad was six-foot-two, steady as a rock, very smart and even-keeled. Mum was gregarious and fun-loving. As the story goes, on their first date, they went out to dinner in Adelaide. Mum is highly allergic to peanuts and accidentally ate some, becoming seriously ill very quickly. Dad took her straight to hospital, and when he went to check her in, he only knew her first name! Fortunately, Mum was okay, and they went on to get married a couple of years later. I was born a year after the wedding. Their marriage is still going strong after more than fifty years, and they love each other dearly.

In my early years on the farm, Mum would have loads of naps. I thought it was because she was depressed from losing the twins. In actuality, she was diagnosed as a celiac when she was sixty, and she now believes that she was so tired when we were kids because she went undiagnosed for so long. A celiac cannot tolerate gluten, which is found in wheat, rye, and barley, and if they eat these foods they become bloated, have stomach troubles, and often are tired and grumpy. Of course, giving birth to five children in the space of four years is bound to have taken a toll on her body as well. My sister was diagnosed as a celiac when she was about five years old, and clearly it is a genetic disease, as two of my sister's children also have the condition. Mum always used to try to make us have afternoon naps until I was seven. We never understood why and we hated naps, but now we know how badly Mum needed to rest!

Mum and Dad used to hang out with the local footballers as Dad was the captain and coach of the team. They used to do this thing they called Eagling. They would randomly turn up to each other's houses in the middle of the night and do wheelies in their cars in front yards, or throw rocks on roofs, and sometimes even sneak into bedrooms and scare the crap out of each other. No one locked their doors in those days; in fact, we didn't even have locks. Mum would wake up from panicked nightmares, often waking Dad saying someone was in the room when no one was there because she was so freaked out by the random scary visits of their mates.

I have also had my share of night terrors and sleepwalking. Off and on throughout my life, I have found myself up and running around the house in the middle of the night, trying to rescue people, stop robbers, or just face scary things. I often sleepwalk during the high-stress times in my life. I am sort of aware that I am doing it, and I am usually in a panic and my heart is pounding. At some point, I wake up and then have to calm myself down and try to go back to sleep. Once, I woke up in the front yard in a panic. Luckily, it was in a safe area and I lived on the ground floor.

Growing up, nearly every year my family went to Wallaroo, a coastal town on the Yorke Peninsula. It has a great beach, but at times the tide can be so far out that we would walk a long way to reach the water. When I was four years old, we were in an old wooden shack situated on the beachfront looking out to sea. A cup of hot tea was left sitting out, and I spilled it on my leg. My parents had to take me off to hospital, and I still have a small dark scar on my leg from the burn. On another trip to Wallaroo, my brother, Sam, who must have been about three, was driving a motorised toy car on the beach on his own. A policeman picked him up and brought him back to the beach shack, where my parents were oblivious to his whereabouts. The policeman said he was too young to be driving along the beach on his own.

Mum said that wherever we went, I would wander off, find a new friend and bring them back to play. Back in the 1970s, parents didn't worry too much about safety and what the kids were up to, so we had loads of freedom to explore and play outdoors. Times have really changed in this day and age with greater safety issues leading to helicopter parenting. Our parents were the opposite, which was great as it fostered our independence, decision-making skills, and creativity. It also meant that my siblings and I had more responsibility for ourselves and others than perhaps we should have.

I was the oldest of all the children of my parents' friends, so sometimes while all the adults were playing at the local tennis club, I was responsible for looking after up to twelve younger children at one time. The tennis club was in the middle of the town and had six grass courts and an old clubhouse where we could buy sandwiches and treats. I loved the cheese and gherkin sandwiches and soft drinks on those hot summer days. The children I looked after would play in the sand pit and climb the ladder to go down the slippery dip and I would keep them all safe and happy for hours. They were always filthy and exhausted by the end of the day, but none of the parents seemed to mind.

Some of these children and their parents went with us to Boomer Beach near Victor Harbour when I was twelve years old. This beach was notoriously rough with huge waves that we used to call dumpers because they would smash you to the ocean floor instead of rolling in smoothly. I would go into the surf alone with two younger girls under each arm. Both little kids would have life jackets on and I was a strong swimmer, but looking back, and with the hindsight that comes with having a child of my own, I am amazed the adults let me out in the wild surf with these young girls. I guess the parents had faith that I would keep them safe. We were very lucky no one drowned.

As kids, we trusted our parents' judgment. They had us believing along with them that the world was a very safe place in the 1970s, and it generally was, but at times it frightened me to think they could be wrong. There were many strange kidnappings and murders in Adelaide during this era, and sometimes this made me question my own safety. Yet, despite my fears, I was friendly, trusting and optimistic about the world and the people in it.

Fun Times in the Country

When I was thirteen, my friends and I were caught by the police drinking and running under the sprinklers on the town oval in the middle of the night. The oval was a big grassy field where Aussie rules football was played each winter. It was right next to the high school, and we held our sports days there every year. I told Mum and Dad about the incident as soon as I got home, so when the police called the next day, they were shocked that my parents already knew. My parents were pretty chilled about it, considering that Dad seemed to act like the local sheriff, even though he was just a farmer. My parents appreciated me being honest, and it's not like they weren't accustomed to having a bit of fun, now and then.

Mum was always easy to talk to when we were kids, and it was natural for us to share with her when we made mistakes or were in trouble. She never really got angry, and we used to have many open and honest conversations about social issues and the things children face growing up. This was so helpful, and I believe it is one reason that my siblings and I are all good communicators as adults. One of the few times I can remember Mum getting mad when I was little is when I swore at her, not realising what I was saying, and she smacked me. I had given her a 'thumbs up' and asked her if she knew what it meant. I told her it was the F word, and she was so cross that she smacked me. I was only smacked a couple of times in my whole childhood, so this was a massive shock considering that I had no idea what I was saying was wrong; I had learned this little gem at kindergarten. Mum also used to yell at us for watching too much television, threatening to put her foot through it. She wanted us to play outside and not get 'square eyes'. Imagine how mad she would have been if we had computers and mobile phones back in those days. It would have driven her crazy!

Dad had a high profile in Riverton and was on every committee you could imagine. He used to walk into the local swimming pool, where I was trying my best to seem cool and get noticed by the hot boys, and would yell at my mates for doing bombs off the diving board. I was so embarrassed and naturally this did not help my street cred at all with the other kids. He had an imposing nature and his booming voice would make me shudder. Dad was a mix of stern and kind, but never mean; he was always fair and consistent.

I had many great adventures growing up. I used to ride my bike for hours around the local hills and visit my girlfriends who lived on the neighbouring farms. My sister, brother, and I would ride a motorised go-kart on a track that my dad had graded through the creek and around the paddock. Dad built us the go-kart out of an old lawn mower engine and a seat from an old chair, welding the rest of it out of scrap metal from around the farm. The kids who lived on the neighbouring farms used to come over and we would all line up to take turns zooming around the farm.

Dad also welded up a sled, and when it rained in winter, we could slide on it down the hill into the creek. Mum and Dad would be entertaining friends in the house and all of the kids would head out to ride the sled down the slippery, wet hill. We used to get covered in mud from head to toe, and then run to the front lawn and hose off all the mud before we could go in to have a hot shower. We would be shivering like skinny little beanstalks, but we loved it so much.

It wasn't all fun and games. Dad used to make the three of us go out and hoe thistles in the paddocks at the height of summer. We would have to drive the ute (utility truck) out to the paddock and hoe thistles on our own. The paddock was dry and dusty, with thistles growing as far as the eye could see. It was so hot that in the distance we could see a hazy shimmer over the landscape as the heat danced in front of our eyes. Blow flies buzzed around us and the wooden handles of the hoes left splinters in our hands. I would put the radio on in the ute and lie stubbornly on the bench seat with my feet hanging out of the window, singing along in protest to the Bay City Rollers while my younger siblings did all the hard work. I used to swear at the sky as I would much rather have been back in the house watching 'Bewitched' or 'The Brady Bunch.' My behaviour on these trips to hoe thistles is still a hot topic at family events. Dad thinks it is hilarious that I hated it so much, yet I had no choice.

One of the other life lessons the farm gave me was how to fight fires, which were common in the Australian summer heat. They were something that required the whole family's help whilst we waited for the fire truck and the neighbours to join the fight. Dad would fly into action, and I would be at his side like a chip off the old block. We would be hard at work, giving commands, getting supplies, and running to the front line of the fire to literally beat it out with hessian grain bags. Meanwhile, Mum and my siblings ran around like chooks with their heads cut off. I can see now that these fires were a great training ground for me to learn to act swiftly in any emergency.

One steaming hot summer's day, I was sitting on the stone veranda outside the local pub while Dad was inside having a beer. The town fire siren started wailing, the pub doors flew open and every bloke inside ran out, jumped in their vehicles and drove off to fight the fire. It was such a heart-warming feeling to see a whole community rally to help. This fire was right behind my Nan's house, so I was even more relieved to see the fire extinguished quickly. Most of the farmers had water tanks and hoses ready for action on the back of their utes during the summer so they could fight a fire at a moment's notice. Fires were constant events in this town; after all, we were living 'in the driest state, on the driest continent on earth', according to a television commercial warning us to conserve water in the 1970s.

I learned to drive at a very young age and was steering a truck or ute at the age of four and by six was driving alone on the farm. When I was about four, I was steering the old Bedford truck while Dad was on the back feeding hay to the sheep. He put the truck in first gear and told me to steer in a straight line down the hill. As I was alone in the cabin doing what he asked, he was on the back throwing hay to the hungry sheep gathering around. I looked at the pedals below me and wondered what they were for. I put my foot down on the far right one and suddenly the truck lurched forward, Dad flew off the back, and I started careening down the hill alone towards the creek.

I was freaking out as I had no idea what was going on or how to stop the truck. Dad jumped up and ran like a champion to catch the truck. He swung the door open and slammed his hand on the brake, saving me from crashing into the creek. He then started to yell at me, obviously panicking and scared for what might have happened if he didn't catch me. Even at that age, I remember feeling quite indignant because if he had just taken the time to tell me what the pedals were for and to not touch them, then I would have left them alone and we wouldn't have been in that predicament.

My sister nearly drowned a few times when I was young. We were at the house of Mum's friend Grace and my sister, who was about eighteen months old, fell into the fish pond and started going up and down under the water with her big terrified eyes gazing up at me. I was only three, yet I ran inside and said, 'Mum, Mum, Nikki is in the fish pond!' Mum rushed into the lounge room to look for her, as she thought that I had said that Nikki had fallen into the fireplace. I yelled, 'No, no, the fish pond!' and Mum raced out the front door and pulled my sister spluttering and crying out of the fish pond. Soon after, Grace had mesh netting put over the pond.

Another time my parents were at a friend's palatial house in Adelaide and the adults were socialising and playing tennis while the kids were in the pool. Mum had just given birth to my brother Sam and was breastfeeding him while my sister and I were playing in the pool. I must have been five and Nikki would have been three years old. Nikki was floating in a rubber ring and I was able to swim. Suddenly, Nikki flipped upside down in the rubber ring and was stuck with her legs flailing in the air. I ran to Mum and said, 'Mum, Mum, Nikki is upside down in the swimming pool!' Mum bellowed in panic to Dad, who was playing tennis nearby, and like a superhero all kitted out in white, he flung his tennis racquet up in the air and leapt like a gazelle into the pool and saved my sister from certain death.

The final time my sister nearly drowned, she was almost four and we were at the local swimming pool. I was tall and could swim, she was short and could not. I pushed her out of her depth and she began sinking to the bottom, but I had a change of heart and rescued her. Strangely enough, I am responsible for saving my sister three times.

I went to the local kindergarten when I was three years old. I was a confident kid and loved being at kindy. All the activities were so entertaining and creative, and I enjoyed hanging out with the other kids. One day, I thought I would be clever and write my name in red crayon on the wall of the changing room. I wrote 'Julie' with a back-to-front J. Later, one of the kindy teachers came up and told me off for writing on the wall. I was completely stumped. I could not work out how they knew it was me. It seems I was not the sharpest knife in the drawer!

In grade one, my friend convinced me to leave school and go to her house during the school day. It was in the middle of summer and a stinking hot day. When we arrived at her house, I became ill. Her mum was there and looked after me. It turned out that I had sunstroke and was quite unwell. We got in trouble for leaving school, and on top of that, I was very queasy and spaced out. Though I didn't have the words yet for the concept, I felt like it was my karma for breaking the rules, and I never bunked off school again.

In year seven, my last year of primary school, I got a handwritten valentine note drafted in red pen and soaked in a hideous perfume. It was from someone professing their love for me and saying that they wanted to do to me what Jim and Lisa would do at the back of the picture theatre in town. Eeek, I was so freaked out! This proclamation of undying love came a little too early in my life for me to appreciate it. It made some unusual and unrecognisable feelings stir within me, and that made me feel uncomfortable. I never discovered who wrote the note. It remains the only thing I have received for Valentine's Day in my entire life.

I had crushes on boys throughout primary school, but never a boyfriend. Boys always seemed to want to play sport with me or be my mate, but nothing more. This seemed to set the tone for the rest of my life: I have the 'buddy curse.' I've always had many male friends but very little romance. I think I made that term up, but it has been a theme in my life where I have had so many wonderful male friends but very few partners. This has partly added to my sense of inadequacy, which I try to keep well hidden, and has made me question deep down whether something is wrong with me. In my early twenties, a psychic told me I would be surrounded by men and have loads of great friends, but that real love would always be out of reach. I remember thinking at the time how sad it would be to be alone for most of my life, but I was hopeful that she was wrong. Now it is very clear to me that she was spot-on.

Teen Years

I had a fabulous time at high school in Riverton, and was such a social creature that I didn't ever want to have a day off sick as I was afraid of missing out on fun with my friends. This was FOMO (fear of missing out) in the eighties before the term was invented. When I did have to miss school because I was sick with the mumps or chicken pox, I would stay at home, lying on the couch, drinking flat lemonade and watching old midday movies on TV. I used to particularly love watching Sidney Poitier and Elvis movies. Both of these guys were so handsome and talented that I developed a teen crush on them, the first of many in my lifetime.

I was a super-sporty girl and loved to be involved in as many activities as I could, like dance and school productions. I was friends with most of the kids, but I was bullied at school by one mean boy, Allan. He used to call me 'pirate's delight' (sunken chest) or 'carpenter's delight' (flat as a board and easy to screw). He used to walk up and rub his hand on my shoulder or down my back where a bra should have been and then laugh at me because I was not wearing one. I had not developed boobs, like most of the other girls had, and was very flat-chested. The bullying really upset me, but I did my best to brush it off and try not to show that I was embarrassed and uncomfortable with these comments. I was tall, skinny, and a late developer; I didn't develop breasts or have my period until I was fifteen. Once, feeling particularly down in the dumps and different from my peers, I asked Mum if I was a boy, even though I knew I wasn't. She was surprised but gently reassured me that I was just a late bloomer and would develop soon enough. I feel so lucky that I was comfortable having this conversation with Mum and that she took me seriously, responding with compassion that helped me navigate such a tumultuous time.

I felt hurt by the bullying, but it didn't have a serious impact on me and I remained confident and sociable. Thank goodness there were no mobile phones or internet in those days. At least back then, bullying was contained in the schoolyard, and once you left school and went home you were relatively safe.

Mum and Dad often used to go to parties at people's farms and stay until the early hours. All the kids would play out and about until dark, and when it was bedtime we would all sleep in the back of the family station wagon. I used to love being driven home asleep in the back of the car. The hum of the engine and the rocking motion was so comforting, and I would feel so cosy and safe. This continued until I grew too tall for us all to fit, and then we had to get babysitters.

As I grew older, I was the babysitter. One of the kids in our neighbourhood troupe was a girl, Kelsey, who lived next door to our farm. She was six years younger, so I often went to their place to babysit the three children while her parents went out in town. One night, I was looking after them when Kelsey called out from her bedroom. I went to check on her and her whole face was swelling up, and it looked like some kind of allergic reaction. She could feel her throat getting tighter, and I was worried that it would close up and she would not be able to breathe.

I ran to the medicine cabinet looking for antihistamines, but couldn't find any. I didn't have a number to call her parents, and there were no mobile phones in those days. I decided to ring Mum, who was at home only about a mile away. She drove over with some antihistamines and was able to get hold of Kelsey's parents. They rushed home and took her to hospital, where she was given an injection to stop the allergic reaction. They never found out what made her swell up like that, and it never happened again.

One day, whilst on my parents' friend's farm, I was the oldest child in the group as usual and was leading our troupe around the farm. There was an old abandoned house called the White House at the top of a hill. It was rumoured to be haunted, and I was spooking all of the kids out as I led them up the hill to the house to look for ghosts. I was thirteen and the kids behind me were all ages, right down to three years old. I led them in single file like the Pied Piper on a mission, right up to the old house. The garden was overgrown with grass that we had to wade through to get to the door of the garage. The windows were filled with dust and cobwebs. We could hear the bold, loud cries from the galahs in the gum trees surrounding the house, daring us to go in. The mood was tense, as we expected to see a ghost at any moment, and the air was still and hot. I slid the bolt back, pulled open the garage door, and right in front of me was a huge old sheep, staring at me face to face. It bleated *Baaaaaaaaaaaa* extremely loudly and I screamed and peed my pants in fright. All of the kids behind me were hysterical with laughter, and I had to lead them, embarrassed, back down the hill to the farmhouse so I could change my pants. So much for being large and in charge.

One of the kids closest to my age in this troupe was a boy named Chris, who lived at the farmhouse we were visiting. He used to dare me to do reckless things, as he was a bit of a prankster, and often I would do them, even though I knew they were not a good idea. He'd encourage me to touch an electric fence or ride a horse bareback when I was not skilled at riding. He used to take me roaring around the farm on the back of a motorbike, and one day an electric wire had fallen down at eye height across a dam. He drove straight towards it around the edges of the dam at great speed. Luckily, I saw it coming and was able to duck down quickly before it decapitated me.

On another evening, a large group of children were staying at my house while our parents were a mile away at a neighbour's party. Chris and I were waltzing around in the kitchen and messing about while the younger children were watching and laughing at us. Suddenly, we bumped into the wooden extender plank of the dining table that was leaning up against a wall. It fell in slow motion and smashed the beautiful, original stained-glass door that joined our kitchen and lounge room. We froze, all looking at one another and then at the coloured glass all over the floor. My heart sank. Chris and I were meant to be the responsible ones. I thought we were going to be in so much trouble.

I built up the courage and rang the next-door neighbours to break the news to my parents. Someone answered the phone, I asked for my dad and said it was an emergency. The parents were partying down in the barn, so someone had to run down to find Dad and give him the message. He raced to the phone, worried something disastrous had happened. When I told him we had smashed the beautiful old stained-glass door, he was so relieved that the house was not on fire—and that nobody was injured, or worse—that he was not even upset. I was relieved, too, and began to internalise the message that my parents were level-headed and fair, and that my life mattered far more than our possessions.

Unrequited Love

My penchant for dark-skinned men began to develop in my early teens when I watched films starring Sidney Poitier, my teen celebrity crush. I also fancied Elvis, so I never fancied darker-skinned men exclusively, but I do trace my interest in them back to good old Sidney. He was tall and suave, and I loved the way he dressed in suits. Sidney always seemed to be gazing intently at me through the TV screen. There was something about his full lips and white teeth that made my heart flutter.

I got drunk for the first time when I was fourteen. I was at my friend's house at a party that her older brothers were throwing. I drank too much and ended up sleeping in one of her brothers' empty bunk beds and throwing up in it. I felt sick the next day and embarrassed. I was worried about my dad finding out and that I'd be in loads of trouble. Apparently, Dad heard about the party at the local pub the next day. Nothing is sacred in a small town where everyone knows everyone else's business. Luckily, he wasn't too mad at me and more or less made fun of the situation instead. That was a huge relief. I would love to say I learned my lesson and did not do it again, but unfortunately that is not the case.

I had a massive crush on a boy named Marc, and this lasted for years. We were good friends, but nothing more. He dated two of my best friends while I was always the third wheel—the story of my life, really. Finally, at the end of year ten, just before I was to leave Riverton and go to the big smoke to boarding school, I hooked up with Marc at a teen disco in the local town hall. We ended up snogging for a couple of hours. This was my dream come true and my first intimate, passionate experience and I loved it. I consider him my first real infatuation and he was an awesome, sexy guy. He sparked feelings in me that I had never experienced. I had a diary for a couple of years in which I wrote about my unrequited love for him. So, to actually get to kiss him was a dream come true and very exciting. It's amazing how intense teen love can be and the emotions it can evoke.

Not every experience that I had with dating guys was as thrilling as the one I had with Marc. Around this time, I went on a date with a guy who was a bit older than me. He was from a nearby town, and somehow I ended up staying the night, in a separate room, at his parents' place. In the middle of the night, I woke up to find him on top of me and trying to force me to have sex. I was still a virgin and did not want to have sex, but he was trying to pry my legs apart. I held my legs together in a vice-like grip, using all the strength I had, and I told him in no uncertain terms that if he did not get off me, I would scream for his mother to come and help me. Luckily, this worked, and he went back to his bedroom. I was so relieved and glad I had kept my wits about me. I am sure my physical strength, my forceful nature, and a dose of good luck possibly stopped me from being raped that night. I never saw him again.

Boarding School

It was a longstanding family tradition throughout the generations that the boys went to boarding school, not the girls, but Mum changed all that. She was determined that the girls in the family would have the same opportunities as my younger brother, Sam. This was my first taste of feminism and it also supported the positive way I was brought up: to be whatever I wanted, and to grow into an independent, strong woman. My sister and I were told we must have our own careers and we should not rely on a man to support us. I am so thankful that Mum was a progressive thinker when I was young and that this spirit of independence and feminism seeped into my soul.

I went to a girls' boarding school in Adelaide for the last two years of high school. It was a beautiful old establishment, originally built in the early 1880s as a hospital and then became a school in the early 1900s. It consisted of magnificent ornate, high-ceilinged stone architecture, well-manicured gardens and was one of the most prestigious girls' schools in the city.

I loved my time as a boarder and excelled at sport, particularly swimming, athletics, and netball. I won medals in swimming and athletics, and I captained both the netball and basketball teams. I was not so brilliant at basketball because I was a bit uncoordinated at dribbling whilst running; however, my height under the ring made up for my lack of agility down the court. I made lots of friends, and after a year as a boarder, I was voted Vice House Captain and Boarding House Prefect. This was a huge honour, and I took my roles very seriously and was proud to be in these leadership positions. I led sports day and swimming carnival events, represented the boarding house in relay races, and loved the annual house choir competition. I fully immersed myself in all that boarding school had to offer, and it helped build my character in so many positive ways.

However, for the first three months I spent at boarding school, I was quite homesick. It was my first time away from home, and despite my confident and outgoing nature, I missed it. Recently, Dad found a letter I wrote to Nan when I was at school. In the letter, I complained that I missed sleeping in, as I had to wake up early every day and was not used to it. I said was looking forward to coming home to my lovely bed and Nan's bathtub, but that I missed Mum the most.

Some of the best times were during whole school assemblies in the majestic old hall, where the light shone through the ornate windows and gave the room a feeling of reverence. In one assembly, my friend Ava and I did a performance of a show that was popular in Australia at the time, 'Young Talent Time.' This weekly variety program featured talented teenagers who would sing and dance. Ava played Johnny Young, the host, and she called me up—'Little Julie Hannaford!'—out of the audience and onto the stage. She sang 'You Light Up My Life' to me in an exaggerated Aussie accent while I sat on her knee. I remember looking at the audience rollicking with laughter in their seats as the performance went on. I absolutely loved performing and the adrenaline rush it gave me.

I dressed in a suit and carried a violin case onstage in front of the whole school during another assembly. I was very serious and looked like I was about to perform a classical music piece. I got to the lectern and microphone, opened the violin case, and pulled out a pen and a bottle of Liquid Paper. I put the bottle in my mouth and proceeded to play the song 'Popcorn' on the bottle with the pen, creating the musical notes by moving my mouth around. This is still a great party trick that I pull out every once in a while. Once again, I had the audience in stitches.

Another time, I organised the boarders to create a parody of 'The Brady Bunch', calling it 'The Boarding Bunch.'

Each family member was played by a lookalike boarder with a similar hair style. I played Greg Brady and was caught by Marsha and Jan having my first shave without telling Dad. I had shaving cream all over my face and used the audience as my 'mirror', shaving with a real razor with the cap still on it. The whole family had to have a meeting to decide if I was allowed to shave. After a family debate in true 'Brady' style, it was decided that I was permitted to shave and hence my rite of passage to becoming a man had been ratified by the family. The play was a huge success and was hilarious. In hindsight, I might have missed my calling to work in comedy. I did, however, spend many years as a drama teacher, so I used these skills later in life and found my calling in many ways.

My natural leadership skills were starting to develop in the supportive school environment. However, it was also here that I had my first real taste of rebellion and risk-taking. I was testing the waters with fairly mild mischief, like dressing in pyjamas on the last day of school and having flour fights or getting drunk at a school dance that I organised. I was caught drinking at the dance with Ava, who, dressed as a nun, had jumped on me in the bathroom earlier in the night, chipping my front tooth. I crawled around in pain on the bathroom floor searching for the missing piece of the tooth, but I could not find it. I patched the chipped tooth with Blu Tack until I could get to the dentist to get it fixed. The Blu Tack stopped the pain by preventing air or water from touching my broken tooth. After the bathroom incident, Ava, who was even drunker than me, was caught by a teacher and ended up passed out in the Headmistress's office.

Several of us were called to talk to the Headmistress and the Head of the Boarding House, Dibley, who was like a wizened old witch. We gathered together in a little room next to the boarding house kitchen, standing in a semicircle and struggling to maintain focus due to having skulled the best part of a bottle of Brandavino in the park next to the school before staggering into the dance. We had purchased the alcohol after dinner on the way back to school, where the dance was being held. We were all dressed up and mucking around in the parklands across the road from the school before the dance began.

I remember the room swaying a bit and having to work hard to hold it together. The Headmistress sniffed a package of chocolates that Ava had in her bag and asked us if there were any drugs involved. Being the bold girl that I was, and rather drunk as well, I slurred back to her, 'Miss White, I can guarantee you there were no drugs involved.' She replied in an acidic tone, 'Julie Hannaford, you are in no position to guarantee anything.' As we had all denied drinking, and obviously held it together just enough to fool them, a frustrated Miss White decided to let us go.

As we left the room, I held the door open for the other girls to exit and just stood there like a defiant fool, giving Miss White the hairy eyeball as the others marched, albeit a bit wonkily, out the door. As I glared at the Headmistress, she slowly lifted her finger and beckoned me to come back. Oops, my goose was cooked! Dibley dragged me with her hawkish talons to bed upstairs in the boarding house as the disco continued below us in the large assembly hall.

Once alone, I had an idea. I staggered to the nerdy girls' room—two shy, quirky girls who hadn't gone to the dance—to borrow sixty cents. I was planning to escape from the boarding house to ring my mum to come and rescue me. In my drunken state, I thought sixty cents would be enough for the call and that Mum would come to my rescue this late at night when she lived fifty miles away on the farm.

I took my sixty cents and went back to my room to think. I was still determined to call Mum, so I tried the doors to the bedroom wing. I had been locked in! Undeterred, I jumped out of the second-floor window and lay commando-style flat on my back on the veranda roof with the sixty cents clutched tightly in my hand. The boarding house was a big old two-story Australian colonial building with high ceilings and a veranda running all the way around it. I crab-crawled sideways across the veranda like an inebriated ninja and jumped back in through the kitchen window on the first floor. I stumbled down the stairs and hid behind the exit door, trying to gather my senses. As I was contemplating my next move, which was to run outside and jump the back fence of the school and go and call Mum from a phone booth, I paused to try to focus. Just as I was about to embark on the final leg of my mission, I was busted by the father of another student who was there to help supervise the dance. It just so happened that he was also a policeman. I was marched back in to the Headmistress and Dibley, who by then felt like my arch nemesis, and was chastised by them both and marched back to bed for the second time. I gave up and swirled into a deep, drunken sleep.

The next day, I awoke with a cracking hangover and the realisation that I had made some stupid choices and would have to face the consequences. We had to call our parents in front of Dibley and tell them what we had done. Luckily, my parents were fine about it and not upset with me, which was a huge relief. The worst punishment of all was having to wait for a few days to hear what the consequences were going to be. We were very worried that we would be expelled from school in our final year. Eventually, they told me that I was gated (not allowed to leave the boarding house) for nine weeks, which ended up being only four weekends on lockdown, as holidays and exeats (weekends when we were all out of the boarding house) were included in the nine weeks. I faced my sentencing with dignity, but I can't say I learned from it.

One night, we were upstairs in the boarding house watching dear old Miss White, the Headmistress, walking across the school grounds. Another girl and I flashed our bums at her out of the windows as she walked towards us and sent the whole common room into hysterics. Miss White stormed upstairs to confront the flashers, but we all denied any knowledge of the incident, and as she couldn't very well identify us from our bums, we got away with it.

Once, when we had an exeat and all went home from school, I took three girls with me to stay on the farm. That Saturday night, we went to a disco in the neighbouring town. We had a great night and a few drinks, but we didn't go mad, and we flirted with some boys who were a year older than us.

The next morning, I was driving the girls through the town. As we were going down the main street, we could see some of the lads we hung out with the night before driving towards us. As it was a Sunday morning, the town was deserted, and it was just our cars heading towards each other. Suddenly, the boy driving decided to play chicken, moving onto the same side of the road. We were heading towards each other, and the idea was to see who would pull away first.

I was not up for this at all. I was only sixteen, driving Dad's car, and did not want to be a part of this stupid game. I could see a side road coming up on my right, so I turned to go down a side street to avoid a head-on collision. At the same time, the boy driving the other car moved back into his rightful lane, and he smashed all down the side of my dad's blue Ford. Luckily, we were all wearing seatbelts, and no one was hurt. Our cars came to rest right outside a local policeman's house. Strewth!

The policeman, who heard the collision, came out of the house still in his pyjamas and checked to see if we were ok. He got dressed and hauled us around the corner to the police station and called Dad and the boy's parents to come and get us. I felt sick to my stomach and beside myself with fear that Dad would be furious and I was going to be in loads of trouble. He was always a pretty strict father when we were children, with a very commanding presence. I was wary of him as a teen, as he seemed to have pretty high expectations from my perspective.

Nervously, I waited for Dad to arrive. When he finally walked into the police station, he said, 'Are you alright? We were so worried. We can replace the car, but we can't replace you.' I was shocked. Who was this man, and where was my dad? I had not expected this compassionate, loving, and understanding approach, even though that is really what he is like deep down.

Just like the time at the party years ago when he was most concerned about our safety, I took great comfort in his response. I still use this story today as a teacher to calm my students if they have made a massive mistake to show them that parents love their children first and foremost and will not always respond in the way their kids might expect. I made a deal with myself to be like that when I grew up and became a parent.

Being a Crown Up

Out in the World

Despite my desire to go to university, Mum pushed me to get a job in a bank and leave high school before my final term ended. I don't know if she thought I was not bright enough to go to university, or not responsible enough. Perhaps she thought banking was a good career for a girl who hates maths, is useless with numbers, and is much more creative, theatrical, and sporty. Who knows what she was thinking? I drew the line at quitting before the term ended, I completed my final exams and happily passed Matric (year twelve) by five points!

After a year of boredom as a bank teller, I realised taking this job was a big mistake, as I suspected it would be. I used to pretend to not understand the assigned tasks so that others would do them for me. My heart really was not in banking; I was busy enjoying my first year out of school and attempting to be an adult. I can't say that I was very successful at either, but I was enjoying my freedom from boarding school and earning my own money, so life felt pretty good.

I had my first boyfriend during this stage and lost my virginity with him at the age of seventeen. He was a nice enough guy, but a little boring and bland. We met in the bank and moved into a share house together with about eight other people in Walkerville, which was a real hoot. I broke up with him after a couple of years because I didn't really fancy him anymore, although he was a decent bloke who was quite harmless and treated me well.

After a year of this unsuitable career, I decided that I wanted to study further, so I started a Bachelor of Arts majoring in communications at a university in Adelaide and went on to a postgraduate in teaching. I loved university life and had a great time socialising. I did enough work to pass all of my subjects, but I was not a high achiever. I was not overly motivated by academic success, and I am sure, in hindsight, that I was capable of achieving so much more. I spent a lot of time sitting down by the creek with my mates smoking and having a laugh, while the good students were in lectures.

To make ends meet, I worked in nightclubs and bars. I had a great time and enjoyed a pretty raucous and hectic lifestyle. I worked for a number of years in a funky nightclub called Lux for a bunch of Italian guys who owned it. This was the eighties, and we were in the heart of Adelaide's music scene. These were heady days of partying, dancing, and working into the early hours of the morning.

Our bosses at Lux were awesome and really looked after us and treated us like family. It kind of felt like they were part of the Mafia, but this was really just because of their pseudo-gangster lifestyle, which had us young girls in awe. They appeared to have lots of money and connections, acting like they were totally cool and in charge. I have no idea how connected they were or what kind of activities might have been going on, but to me, a girl from a country town and fresh out of boarding school, it felt like we were in the epicentre of the Adelaide underworld.

One New Year's Eve, the club was pumping, full of people, and hot eighties tunes were filling the smoky room. Suddenly, the owner of Club Ka, a bar next door, hit one of my bosses over the head with a bottle of champagne and they started fighting. They were both about five-foot-two, and I am six feet. I strode in and just put my arms around my boss and pulled them apart, like two scrapping kids. I stood in the middle of them like an Amazon woman, holding them apart with ease until they stopped fighting.

During my nightclub days, I was also modelling and acting to make extra money. I worked on a TV series called

'Pals', where I played a 'bimbo called Barbie' (my character description in the script) who was injured in a car accident. I can still remember my lines. I had such a great time working on this series, as the cast were wonderful people, the director was a good friend of mine, and we were required to shoot on location all over South Australia, so it was a real adventure.

I also worked on a film called 'The Time Guardian' that was shot in an old quarry in the Adelaide hills, and there were pyrotechnics and explosions all over the place. I was an extra who wore a cyborg suit. You had to be six feet tall to fit into the suit, and there was one female cyborg lead actor, so I was her stand-in, along with one other girl who was also tall. We had a fabulous time making this film, especially as there were so many 'cyborgs' who bonded whilst sitting around waiting for each scene to be set up for a new shot. Working on a film can be quite tiresome because there is a lot of down-time between shooting scenes, so having a lot of hilarious, outgoing people to hang out with made the time pass much more quickly.

Once, I modelled in a fashion show at a popular Adelaide club. Up until this point, I had done a few fashion parades, but given that I was still only about nineteen with very little experience walking in high heels, fashion modelling was not very easy for me. In fact, Mum enrolled me in a modelling course for a week during the holidays when I was a gawky, skinny fifteen-year-old, and I felt a bit like a fish out of water. However, the skills I learned during that course were very helpful when I started modelling and acting after high school.

During this fashion show, I was dancing with my friend Jerry, and as I danced backwards, I crashed into the set and fell over. There were about four hundred people watching, and I just went down like a sack of potatoes. Jerry kindly helped me up, and despite my face going red and my heart beating out of my chest, we continued on with the show. Once it was over, I vowed never to do a fashion show again as it was just too humiliating! That was the last show I ever did.

Married Young

While working at Lux, I met an Australian-born Yugoslavian/Russian bouncer named Goran who was working at another nightclub. He was nine years older, tall, confident, and outgoing. He had long, 'new romantic' style dyed blond hair and seemed very hip. I was only nineteen, but so ready for this grown-up world of dating and clubbing—or so I thought.

We spent a few months dating whilst working at our respective clubs, and then he got a job as a bouncer at Lux. We were living a flashy lifestyle, seeing amazing bands and partying with lots of cool people in the eighties club scene. I remember seeing Goran lose his temper with customers at the club while working on the door, and more than once he was involved in fistfights that resulted in bleeding and injuries. I brushed aside my concerns about his temper and carried on dating him. I either didn't recognise the red flags or just didn't trust my instincts.

Goran owned a house in Adelaide, and eventually I moved in. It was a prefabricated house and wasn't in a great area, but to me, this was a very grown-up move, and he seemed to be a sophisticated man as opposed to the boys I had previously dated. The house was on a large block of land and had a lovely garden, as he was a keen gardener. Inside the house was a bit run-down and full of retro furniture and lots of knickknacks, as he seemed to be a collector of random odds and ends.

Goran's dad offered to pay off the rest of the money owed on his house if he agreed to marry me. The idea of having his house paid off seemed to be appealing, so Goran asked me if I wanted to get married. I knew about the offer, but I quashed any negative thoughts, ignored my intuition, and went along with it. It stands to reason that this is not a great way to start a marriage, when your boyfriend's father is bribing him to propose and it was not his idea. I am not sure why I said yes; maybe because I wanted to be more grown-up than I really was. We got married in a park just before I turned twenty-two.

The wedding was great. Our friend played Bon Jovi on the guitar during our wedding ceremony, and everyone drank champagne and mingled in a stunning, beautifully manicured park. The ceremony was non-denominational so it was quick and simple. Goran's parents were not impressed that he was not getting married in the Yugoslavian church. To please them, we had tried to arrange that, but the priest would not accept us because Goran said he was not religious. His parents came to the park wedding, put on a brave face and seemed to enjoy the day. The reception was at Lux nightclub. The owners kindly gave us the venue for free, and we had a ska band from Melbourne. It was full of our friends and everyone danced the night away. Despite the fact that someone stole Mum's purse, which put a bit of a dampener on the event, it was a great success. Sadly, this was a lovely beginning to a nightmare marriage.

We went to Bangkok for our honeymoon. It was on this trip that I realised I had made a mistake by marrying him. He was not very nice to people we interacted with, he was impatient and lost his temper over small things. He got ill on the trip and became demanding, sending me off alone around the foreign city to try and buy medicine for him. More and more, I was realising that I did not feel entirely at ease with him. Sometimes, it's not until you travel with someone that you see the real person, and I didn't like what I was seeing. A subtle, nagging worry was rising slowly in the pit of my stomach.

Over the years with Goran, I would often feel uncomfortable and embarrassed by his arrogant attitude and behaviour. It was as if once we were married, he didn't have to try so hard and could be his true self, and this side of him was not very appealing. He was quite a know-it-all and would often dominate conversations with friends, making sure they were aware that he was the most knowledgeable on any topic of discussion. Sometimes, I would cringe in silence at the way he spoke to others. I felt out of my depth in the marriage, but I was too young and naïve to do anything about it.

My marriage was as tumultuous as it was short-lived. Goran used to punch holes in the walls, throw things, rant and rave, and carry on like a lunatic. He would get furious with me if I did not rinse the dishes after I washed them, or if I did not hang the clothes on the line in a particular way. He was pedantic about how his clothes should be folded, or how his piles of old newspapers were stacked. If things were not done correctly, he would yell and scream at me. One time, we were having an argument in the hallway, and he got so frustrated that he punched three holes in the wall right next to my head. I was intimidated and afraid, but I felt if I could just be a better wife, I could change him. I wasn't aware at the time that often violent behaviour is repeated and that many abusive men don't change without professional help.

I had not grown up in a family with this kind of behaviour, so it was all completely new to me and I did not know how to deal with it. I soon discovered that a passive, meek approach was the quickest way to de-escalate his yelling or abusive behaviour. Sometimes my passivity provoked him and he would tell me that I was stupid, and the more I heard that, the more it started to become ingrained in me as the truth. I started to question my level of intelligence and felt that he must be superior because he was smarter. He probably wasn't smarter than me, but I started to believe it. This behaviour is called *gaslighting*: a form of manipulation where the aggressor revises the past and makes you question reality, and even your own sanity. This tactic makes the person doing it feel more powerful and in control, at the expense of the power and control of the victim. Back then, I didn't know this term or concept. To me, it was just abusive behaviour that I did not have the skills or maturity to deal with. He wore me down over time with his verbal abuse and violent outbursts, and I gradually began to lose my confidence and sense of self.

Not long after we got married, I came home after work a bit drunk, as I had partied with my girlfriend after my waitressing shift. I left my diaphragm out, and my husband and I had sex. This was a fortuitous mistake because it was the beginning of a new chapter in my life with the greatest thing that has ever happened to me: my child. I married Goran knowing that he did not want children and I did; a total recipe for disaster, but the real disaster was that he did not feel any joy in what we had created.

Despite my growing misgivings at being married to my moody and petulant husband, I pushed my concerns away and continued on with daily life, unaware of the new life inside me. A few weeks later, after work, I decided to meet my friends at a bar nearby at about midnight. As I came around the corner of the block, I could see that there had been a car accident and someone was lying on the road with a group of people surrounding him trying to help.

As I got closer, I realised that it was my friends who were trying to help him. I rushed over and I could see that my mates were all a bit shocked and also a bit drunk, and did not know what to do. I had just come from work and was sober, so I took control of the situation. Two of my friends were nurses, so we all got to work. He wasn't breathing. I felt for a pulse, and there was none. He did not have a mark on his body but had obviously been hit by the car as the windscreen was smashed.

I told someone to call an ambulance and we started giving CPR. I was doing the breathing and the other two girls were taking turns to do the chest compressions. At one point I could hear a rattling sound in his chest. I knew it was likely to be the death rattle, and I thought he was not going to survive, but we continued on regardless, waiting for the ambulance to arrive. At this moment, amongst all the chaos and emotion swirling around us, I had a premonition that I was pregnant.

46

My period was not even due yet, but as I was giving CPR to this guy, I suddenly knew in my heart I was going to have a baby.

The next day, I woke up and I realised that I had shards of glass in the roof of my mouth. Even though the accident victim didn't have a mark on his body, he must have inhaled slivers of glass when he hit the windscreen. I heard on the news that he had not survived, which I already suspected. I called Mum to tell her about the night before. She was worried that I may have contracted HIV, so she called the coroner to see if the accident victim was HIV positive. The results showed that he didn't have it. This was in the late eighties and HIV was all over the news at the time and in advertising campaigns that instilled fear in the public, so I understood her concern.

To get the glass taken out of the roof of my mouth, I had to go to the emergency room because it was a Sunday. Eventually, a doctor saw me, and he started brusquely picking around my mouth. I could feel the tweezers clinking on the glass. 'The roof of your mouth is very fibrous, so this is not going to be easy,' he said. The next minute, he said there was an emergency and he had to leave, so he just left me there. I was still in a bit of shock from the night before, so I started to cry. I pulled myself together and left the hospital. I drove to my best friend Mari's house and burst into tears as I walked in. She sat me down and tweezed about eight slivers of glass out of the roof of my mouth. There was only one that she could not get and it is still there to this day.

On Monday, I decided to go to the doctor for a pregnancy test. I had not forgotten the feeling that I had while giving the guy CPR. It came back positive. I was thrilled and a little freaked out as I had not yet missed a period. I was amazed that I had just known, without any doubt, I was pregnant.

I had always wanted to have children and was very excited. I can't say it was the same for my husband, whose behaviour worsened. Once, when I was pregnant and painting the outside of the whole house virtually on my own, Mum came down from the farm to help. As Mum was there, Goran decided

47

he would also help paint, which he generally had done very little of until this point. He started seething over some trivial matter about how we were doing the painting incorrectly. Suddenly, Goran became incredibly angry and bellowed like a beast, threw his paintbrush into the neighbour's yard, and stormed off. I was so embarrassed that he behaved like that in front of Mum, but it turned out to be a good thing, because she was beginning to see what I was putting up with behind closed doors.

Around this time, Mum started to say to me that I didn't have to accept his abusive behaviour and suggested that I could leave to live in a share house owned by my uncle. She told me, 'What he is doing is wrong, and we will come down and help you move.' I know this was a pretty amazing thing for a mother to say to her pregnant daughter in the 1980s, and I am so grateful. She planted the seed in my head that made me realise that I did in fact have a choice, and I did not have to put up with being mistreated and abused.

Despite Mum's encouragement to leave, I stayed with Goran because we were having a child together. I wanted to see if it could work and I kept hoping he would change, so I soldiered on for a while longer. I gave birth to my daughter, the most precious part of my life. I had a home birth (much to my mother's horror) with my friend Mari there, a midwife assisting, and my husband more or less on the sidelines. I had been right into the book 'Spiritual Midwifery', thus I was all about the hippie, home-birthing vibe, and I used breathing and concentration to great effect to manage the pain of my contractions. Mum was not happy that I had given birth at home, but this was understandable given that she had suffered the loss of two babies. I was not very sensitive to this fact, and I only really understood her perspective much later in my life, when I reflected on how her trauma must have made her afraid for me.

Goran irritated me during the labour. At times he was trying to help, but we were just not connecting during the experience, which should be the most magical, loving time for a couple. He was often cooking or working in the garden, so I was not getting the support he should have been able to give. When he was with me during the labour, he was massaging my legs too hard and hurting them, or playing classical music that was making me feel stressed. I still dislike classical music, and when I hear it, those old feelings of irritation rise to the surface.

Having mastered pain management, I had an easy labour. It started at 8 a.m. and I gave birth in the lounge room at 1.17 a.m. the following morning. I found giving birth a bit like a sports day. Each contraction was like a race and I was grateful to get a break in between each one. I had a drug-free home birth, and I did a brilliant job. My daughter was born healthy and without any stress into a calm, loving environment. I was so proud and fell in love with her at first sight. My midwife and my friend Mari were a huge support, and despite feeling irritated with my husband, I wouldn't have had the experience any other way.

After my daughter was born, Goran's mood swings seemed to get worse. Once, I had to go to the toilet urgently and the baby was crying, so I put her in a baby capsule and asked Goran to swing it while I raced to the loo. He was so angry that I had bothered him that he swung the capsule too hard. My daughter fell out of the capsule, landed on her head, and was screaming when I returned. Luckily, she was fine, but I was so upset that he couldn't even help me for a few minutes and ended up hurting our baby in the process. It's not like he was busy at work all day; we had both stopped working in the nightclub. I had started university and was working in a bar. He did not have a job, was home all day and was often very reluctant to help, acting like he was an expert on everything even though he clearly wasn't.

I had only taken three weeks off university when my daughter was born, and I needed to get back to class. I asked Goran, who was still unemployed, to look after the baby, and he reluctantly agreed. When I returned a few hours later, I found the top of the metal heater smashed in. When I asked what had happened, he said that the baby wouldn't stop crying so he punched the heater in frustration. For me, this was the final straw. If I could not leave him alone with our daughter and trust him to take care of her, I knew that I needed to leave to protect us both.

I left him not long after this incident and my parents came to help me move. Having my parents help was brilliant as Goran just had to accept the fact and did not make too much of a fuss. It was very handy to have a tall, imposing father at this time because there was no way that Goran would kick off when Dad was around.

It was wonderful to have my parents' backing; it gave me so much strength and made it much easier to strike out on my own with a ten-month-old baby. Without their permission to leave him, I may not have had the courage or the resources to cope. I am so grateful for their protectiveness and forward thinking, and that they did not have the attitude that I had made my bed and should lie in it. I know that many women dealing with domestic violence are not as lucky as I was to have family support and somewhere to go and live where I would be safe. Even though I know it was the right decision and I learned that when it came down to it, I could protect myself and my daughter, I did not yet know that this was just the beginning of a string of disastrous relationships that would punctuate my life.

Life as a single mother was a challenge, as I was not always able to find someone to look after my daughter and I definitely could not afford childcare. Luckily, I was allowed to take her with me to university and go to class with her in tow, and she was always very well behaved. I often stood up at the back of the lecture theatre swinging her in my arms and even breastfed her in class. I am so grateful for the support that I received from the university and my teachers and know how lucky I was in the early nineties to have this level of access to education.

I finished university with the help of my cousin and her friend who looked after my daughter while I was studying.

When I worked nights in a bar in the city and lived in a share house with up to five people at a time, there were often people at home I could rely on to babysit while I worked. Looking back, I am not sure how, as a young single mother, I continued my studies and worked to make a living at night in bars. Balancing work, motherhood, and study was not easy, but as I was so young, I had a lot of energy, maintained a positive outlook on life, and didn't realise the extent to which I was juggling my responsibilities. I was very good at making the most of the situation, and I believe that, like many mums, I just did what needed to be done to create the best life I could for myself and my daughter.

I am really proud of myself for doing all of that on my own. Even though I was not the best parent, I did my best with the tools that I had at the time. My daughter was never neglected, was well looked-after and loved; I just would have made some different choices if I could do it over again. I would have spent more time at home and put more effort into playing with her and making her my priority. Through all of this drama and the break-up with my husband, his wonderful family have always supported us and made sure my daughter feels that she is a part of their family. I was so lucky to have the support of my family, friends, and university, because without my education, I would not be where I am today.

Striking Out on My Own

As a single mother, I realised that I needed to get a good, steady job that would allow me to provide for my daughter and give me opportunities for a reliable and interesting career. It became clear to me that I could not be a model and an actress, which I had been for a few years during my nightclub days and the early days of university. I had wanted to work in film or television, but now I wanted a career that was consistent and secure. In my mind, a film and television career could not provide me with that. I loved the idea of working with young people and helping shape their lives through education. It was also in my blood to be a teacher, as Mum and her parents were teachers, so it is certainly a family trait and something I had grown up with. I decided teaching was an excellent option because the income was regular and employment opportunities were plentiful, so I studied for my Postgraduate Diploma in Secondary Education the first year that I was a single mum.

I started teaching at a school in Adelaide when my daughter was about two years old. I felt guilty for leaving her, but she adjusted quickly. I think being in childcare enhanced her development on many levels, although in other ways it was difficult, as she was so young to be away from me for long days while I worked. In the childcare environment, however, she was stimulated constantly, which may have contributed to her outstanding intelligence and social skills. It was tough being away from her, but I couldn't see an alternative. I had to make a living to support myself and my daughter.

I immediately found teaching incredibly rewarding. Around this time, I started dating an old friend. While at the all-girls boarding school, he was a student at our 'brother' school and we used to meet up with the boys for dances and events. He is a blues musician with a bit of a tortured soul, and the relationship did not work out—he cheated on me, but we are still friends. We reconnected a few years later, before I left to live in Hong Kong. He wrote a song about me called 'Don't Tell Nobody' about us hooking up again years later because I kept asking him not to say anything to anyone.

Early on in our relationship, when this musician and I were holidaying at my cousin's place on Kangaroo Island, we were outside on the deck of this stunning house on a huge cliff overlooking a beautiful pristine beach with rolling waves. While standing around soaking up the sun and admiring the amazing view, he told me how he was seriously allergic to bees and that he was afraid that he would die if he was stung by one. Suddenly, out of the blue, a bee started buzzing around him and then stung him on his hand. We could not believe that this had happened, and his face went white with fear and shock. Immediately, his whole body started to swell; he went red and blotchy and started to sweat. I could see the fear in his eyes. We were two hours from a hospital in the middle of nowhere.

My cousin called the ambulance to meet us halfway and we threw my boyfriend in the four-wheel drive. I ran to the medicine cabinet to find some antihistamines and thankfully there were some in the cupboard. I gave him four of them and we careened across Kangaroo Island to meet the ambulance. My cousin was driving and I was monitoring my boyfriend, who was lying on the back seat struggling to breathe. I had visions of Radar O'Reilly in 'M*A*S*H' doing a tracheotomy with a pocketknife and a pen and I was seriously worried that I might have to do the same thing. I would have given it my best shot!

It was a very fast, bumpy ride down dirt tracks and things did not look good. He was so swollen from head to toe and could barely breathe. My cousin and I were completely calm and focussed on keeping him alive and getting to the ambulance. Just as I thought I might have to start CPR, the antihistamines kicked in and his breathing started to get a little easier. It was such a relief.

We got to the halfway point and met the ambulance coming towards us with sirens blaring. Thankfully, the worst was over, and he was improving a little. When we got him in the ambulance, I asked them to inject him with something to combat his allergic reaction and the ambulance guys said they were just volunteers and were not able to administer any medications. This was unbelievable, and if I had not given him those antihistamines, I do not think that he would be with us today. He still tells the story of how I saved his life and is eternally grateful to me and my cousin.

Round Two of Domestic Violence

Not long after breaking up with the musician, I started to date Stan, who was the spitting image of Sidney Poitier: tall, dark, and handsome with very similar features. We lived together for five years. We got together when my daughter was two and a half, and he was a great stepdad to her. He had some problems with alcohol and became violent and aggressive when he drank, but I also knew this was the kind of behaviour he had grown up with, so I felt that he didn't know any better. He had also been abused as a child, so I empathised with the rage he felt and which reared its ugly head when he was drinking. Despite his behaviour, I strangely felt able to excuse it because of what I knew about his difficult upbringing—and I was blinded by love.

Goran used to see my daughter intermittently, whenever his new girlfriend arranged a meeting. He showed very little interest in my daughter, but his girlfriend was lovely and my daughter liked her a great deal. After a couple of years, their relationship ended, the visits became fewer and eventually stopped. I applied for full custody of my daughter through the local court and since Goran did not attend the hearing, I was awarded full custody. Goran was not given any visitation rights. This was a relief because I was not convinced that Goran could look after her on his own or control his temper.

On the other hand, Stan treated my daughter very kindly, and I appreciated that. She brought out such a caring and beautiful side to him. When he first met her, she was very shy, and he won her over by creating a friendly character with his hand called The Spider who used to talk to her in an animated voice. He would play with her, help her with things she couldn't manage on her own, make her laugh, and treat her gently. I noticed such a contrast to the way her own father treated her. This was Stan's sweet side, evident whenever my daughter was around, and in the early years of our relationship, it made me fall even more in love with him. Sadly, after a couple of years this relationship took a turn for the worse. He hit me a few times and threatened me many times, stole money from me, and was generally duplicitous. He threw orange juice on the ceiling, smashed things, hid pornography in the shed, disappeared with my car for hours on end, and drank way too much. I still saw so much that was lovable in him, so I stayed hopeful for perhaps too long that the violence would end.

One day, Stan and I watched the film 'Once Were Warriors.' The film is about drinking, dysfunction, and domestic violence. It was like watching parts of my own life on screen. I could see so many parallels in both my relationship with him and my relationship with my ex-husband that the film struck a nerve and made me see what I hadn't been able to see until then. After the film finished, I went into the bathroom and cried my eyes out. I realised that once more, I was caught up in a terrible situation and I had to do something about it, but once again it would take me some time before I made the move to be free again.

There are so many reasons why I took so long to leave both abusive relationships. I was afraid, embarrassed, and ashamed. I had become desensitised to the violence and had low self-esteem, and perhaps most of all was afraid of being alone with a young child. My daughter often had to hide in her room when Stan was kicking off, and even though none of the aggression was directed towards her, she should not have had to witness all that she saw. Once, he was hitting me in my bedroom while my daughter was in the room. She was about four, and I had to tell her to jump into a cupboard and hide, which she did. That I did not leave him sooner is one of my deepest regrets.

Despite the way Stan treated us, I still loved him, and I felt like he really loved me. We were very attracted to each other, and I think that our exceptional sexual attraction also kept me there for much longer than I should have been. Our love and what felt like the physical proof of it gave me hope that I could change him, or that if he loved me enough, he would change for me. I was drawn back into the vicious cycle by his apologies and promises that the violence would end. He always appeared to be genuinely remorseful after each violent outburst, so I gave him many chances to change his ways. I felt that if I could just help him drink less, things would be better.

My daughter loved him and saw him as her stepdad. She was seven and was so heartbroken when we split up; it was a sad time for her, but it was the right thing for me to do, for both of us. I couldn't live like that any longer, and I didn't want my daughter growing up in an environment filled with violence. Although Stan had always been kind to her and treated her well, despite the fighting and tension that she witnessed, it was only getting worse. As the relationship was breaking down, his abuse had escalated to a new and terrible height: he threatened to harm my friends and burn my house down.

I loved him, and stayed for so long because I felt compassion for the struggles he had faced, and for some reason I felt like he needed me to overcome that. The accumulation of years of this behaviour had made me feel that I didn't deserve any better. What I knew for certain was that my daughter did, so I finally packed his belongings and told him to move out.

Expanding My Horizons

Looking for Love Again

I was single for five years after my relationship ended with Stan. I continued working in Adelaide in a couple of different high schools and carried on with my life. I was working hard and enjoying it, but I was alone and it was a struggle to make ends meet financially. My daughter's father never paid any maintenance or offered any financial support for his child. My parents helped me out a bit, but mostly I coped on my own.

I had been feeling lonely, so was glad when my friend Mari and I planned a holiday in Bali. We both had young kids and were single mothers, and we decided to take a week for ourselves while the kids went to stay with their grandparents. At the airport, I saw a very handsome guy who looked like he might be Greek. He noticed me as well, and then, as luck would have it, we discovered were on the same flight to Bali. We started chatting in the airport as we arrived in Denpasar and he agreed to meet us that night in the Sari Bar.

We met up and he and I hit it off. He was studying to be a doctor in Adelaide and was so handsome and smart. We went on day trips together around Bali, and he also joined Mari and I on some of our excursions. In hindsight, I wish I had not left my friend as much as I did but I fell for him hard and fast and I must have lost my sense of reality. At first, it was like something you only see in the movies. This guy and I spent hours just kissing in the pool at his hotel. It was a totally new experience for me and I got swept up in this affair of the heart.

Once we got back to Adelaide, I had my heart set on continuing the holiday romance back home. It was great for the first week or two, but it didn't take long for me to become unhinged about the whole relationship. I had never felt such excitement in a relationship and it messed with my head. I would turn up at his place unannounced and became emotional and slightly obsessive. I don't know what came over me and why I behaved like I did, but I completely ruined it and I understand why he ran for the hills. It was certainly a lesson in self-control and moderation.

I dated another guy who lived near where I worked so I could see him quite often. I kept my cool this time, but it just didn't work out. During a particularly lonely moment soon after, Mum called me to tell me that there were some teaching jobs available in Hong Kong. I thought I had very little to lose and decided to take a leap of faith.

Hong Kong

In 2000, I moved to Hong Kong to teach at an international school. My daughter was eleven years old when we sold our house and most of our possessions and headed off together on this unknown adventure. I was bolstered by the courage that my daughter showed at the prospect of moving to a city in a different part of the world that we knew almost nothing about. If she had said no, I might not have made such a daunting choice.

One of the reasons that I moved to Hong Kong was to try to increase my chances of finding a good man and having a loving relationship. I did not know much about Hong Kong, but I did know that it was quite an international city with people from all walks of life. I thought this would increase my chances of finding love, which I felt was the only thing missing from my life.

I am six feet tall and prefer taller men, so two years before I moved to Hong Kong, when Mum called me to tell me about teaching opportunities there, I replied with pessimism, 'Why would I want to go to a place where I would be the tallest woman in the whole country?' Two years later, she called me again about the same vacancies, but this time I decided the career opportunity was too great to ignore. My initial worries ended up being prophetic, however, and I didn't actually comprehend how much of an impact my height and unwillingness to date shorter men would have on my ability to find someone to share my life with in Hong Kong.

The move to Hong Kong was one of the best decisions I ever made. I have a brilliant job, an amazing lifestyle, and since being here I have been able to travel all over the world. Hong Kong is such a vibrant and eclectic city with a huge cultural diversity. It is both modern and rich in traditional Chinese culture and is often described as a place where East meets West. With its beautiful harbour, skyscrapers, temples, and markets, it is a stunning city that instantly captured my heart and feels like home.

We moved to a small island just to the south of Hong Kong island, where there are no cars and you have to walk or ride a bike to get around. There is a ferry service that connects the island to the main hub of Hong Kong island, and it felt just isolated enough from the madness of the hot, bustling city to feel like a breath of fresh air. There are pathways bordered by tropical plants all over the small island, and its heritage as an area of mainly quiet fishing villages still seeps into the feel of the place. Old Chinese folk tend gardens in the swamps. The frogs sound like cows, and the lush greenery contrasts wildly with the concrete jungle of Hong Kong.

All of a sudden, I was living on what felt like an island paradise, with a job I adored, and I was no longer scraping to get by. I quickly made new friendships by joining the beach volleyball games held every weekend. People from all over the world lived on this island, and I loved mixing with this melting pot of extraordinary people. Learning new customs, hearing unusual accents, and meeting fascinating, vibrant people was just another reason why I fell in love with this place. I gradually built a network of great friends, and I was swept up in a passion for my new lifestyle.

One evening, when my friends and I had all gathered to play board games at my house, my best friend Pam received a call from the police saying that they had arrested her eleven-year-old son. Allegedly, he was throwing bikes off the ferry pier with his friends. Pam was furious. She sprang into action and left the party to run to the police station, which was about a twenty-minute walk. I ran after her to offer support, leaving everyone else behind to continue their game of Trivial Pursuit.

Pam is a great runner and fitness hadn't been my strong suit for a few years. I tried my best to keep up, but I was about to collapse and she was way ahead of me. I grabbed a random bicycle resting against a wall outside a bar in the village and jumped on it to try and catch her.

As I edged closer to her on the bike, my phone rang. It was her son calling me. Her son and I are very close—we used to joke that I played the role of his dad in his life. He knew his mum was on her way and he was worried about the consequences when she arrived on the scene. I guess he was hoping I was coming as well to help ease the tension and offer support to both him and his mum. I answered the phone while I was riding, which is not a good move by any means, and I started to careen towards an old stone wall. With my phone in one hand and the other on the handle bar, I slammed on the brakes and screamed as I flew up in the air, still clinging to the handle bar and the phone. I then stopped in mid-air in suspended animation and flopped back down onto the bike seat. I peed my pants a little in the process (damn my weak pelvic floor).

Pam was just down the bottom of the hill and had heard all the commotion, stopped running, and turned to watch me launch into the air and then drop back down on the bike with a scream. She started to laugh, and that broke the tension and she seemed a little less angry with her son. I called out to her that I had peed my pants and she laughed even harder. My antics on my mission to keep up with her may well have saved her son from his mum's ferocity.

We went to the police station and I sat in the station with a sarong wrapped around me to cover my wet pants. In the end, the kids were let go by the police with a warning, and I returned the bike to the bar. Its owner did not even realise that it was missing. This event is still one of my favourite memories from our early years on the island.

Online Dating

You might wonder, after all of my bad luck with relationships in the past, why I still sought one. I am an optimist and I have never given up hope of finding love. I feel that humans are emotional and spiritual beings who are designed to be in relationships. We crave companionship and love, and I am no different. It can be frustrating and disappointing to see friends finding love and feeling like I am missing out on something important and special. I am a good person with lots of great qualities and I have never understood why I haven't been able to find a loving relationship with someone wonderful.

In my fourth year in Hong Kong, after about nine years of being mostly single, I was on a girls' trip to Boracay in the Philippines. We were all single girls teaching in Hong Kong and went on this holiday together to enjoy the sun, sea, and surf. Many of us were scuba divers, and Boracay is a wonderful island for scuba diving, with an amazing shipwreck just off the coast. On this trip, a perfect environment to lament the lack of good relationships in our lives, a couple of my girlfriends showed me an internet dating site that they had just started using. This was the first time that I had ever heard of the concept of internet dating, but since I had mostly given up on the prospect of meeting a man in Hong Kong the old-fashioned way, I decided to give it a go. As soon as I got home I set up a profile and began the search for my type of man.

I spent hours looking at pictures of men over six feet tall, in my age range, and living in Hong Kong. It didn't take long to realise that my options were very limited, and that I would need to look further afield. I started with China and Japan because they were close by and I figured that a relationship could still be possible across those distances. I came across the same limitations in these countries as well, given my height criteria.

Over the years, many of my girlfriends have challenged me about my choice to date only taller men and questioned why I would make this a deal-breaker and restrict my options. I'd try to explain that dating someone shorter makes me feel gigantic and somewhat masculine. It is hard for me to feel feminine and attractive with someone shorter. I am much more open to dating someone from a different culture than I am dating someone below my height. Even though I fancy olive and dark-skinned men, this attraction is not exclusive; it's just a preference, not a deal breaker.

In addition to darker skin colour, I also fancy men with full lips, broad shoulders, and of course, great height. To me, these men are more masculine, and I find them attractive and unique. This allure to men from faraway lands might be a part of my desire to branch out into the world, to learn more about different cultures, and to perhaps even rebel against society's expectations. Over the years, I have observed that black men tend to be more attracted to me than men of other cultures and backgrounds, as quite often their notion of female beauty aligns more with my body type. I don't fit the mould of the slim, small woman that represents the dominant Western standard of beauty.

As for personality, I look for someone who can make me laugh and is trustworthy, reliable, intelligent, generous, and kind. Most of all, I would like to find someone who thinks I am wonderful and loves me to bits. These were my hopes when I started searching for love online.

Romance in the USA

The first man I met on the internet was Dean from Los Angeles. I purposefully searched for someone who lived in LA as I was going for a summer trip there in 2007 with two girls from work, so I targeted this area on a dating website in the hope of finding Mr Right. Dean was a businessman running a translation service for court cases and the like. He had never been married and was forty years old. I was forty-two at the time and thought that this was a good age difference. We Skyped and emailed for a few months before we met in LA. He was handsome, funny, articulate and seemed like a nice guy. I felt like we had shared enough with each other that I had a good idea of the type of guy he was.

Landing in LA and heading into the city to our hotel was a surreal experience. There were landmarks and buildings everywhere that seemed familiar because I had seen them in the movies and on television over the years. My friends were both Australian as well, and it was our first visit to the USA, so we were all really excited. The hotel was lush, and once we settled in, I gave Dean a call and arranged to meet the next day. My girlfriends were really supportive and encouraging because they cared and were really hopeful that this guy might be someone with whom love could blossom. They didn't like to see me lonely and wanted the best for me.

My two friends and I met up with one of their boyfriends and Dean at Universal Studios. The first thing Dean did was to take us to a bar and buy us all a round of tequila shots. This made my heart sink as I was not a big drinker and I certainly didn't want to date someone who does shots at 11 a.m. I did drink quite a bit in my twenties, but after a few years of this lifestyle, I decided I didn't like the feeling of being excessively drunk or the hangovers, so I cut back on my consumption of alcohol and I have not consumed very much since my early thirties. I pushed my reservations aside and reluctantly joined in.

Later, as we walked around Universal Studios, Dean grabbed me and started to make out with me in front of all and sundry. This freaked me out as we had only met a few hours ago and now he was making a spectacle of us in the middle of a big crowd and in front of my friends. As I was becoming accustomed to doing, I did my best to ignore this feeling of concern. I was flattered that he clearly found me attractive and I was enjoying the attention, but on the other hand, I felt embarrassed that things were escalating so quickly.

Each time we all lined up to go on a ride at Universal Studios, Dean would run off and return with a drink of alcohol. He made me laugh and was charming, if not a bit intense, but generally, everyone seemed to get on well. That night we all went out to dinner. On the way there, he kissed me again in the car in front of my friends. It was too full-on and smelled of desperation. It felt like we were teenagers, in a way that felt immature and slightly awkward.

He became even more inebriated at dinner, and this gave me a sense of foreboding. By this time, I felt ashamed at how he was behaving with my friends. At one point my girlfriend offered to buy everyone a drink and Dean volunteered to go and get them. She gave him $50, and when he returned with the drinks, he did not give her the change. I didn't notice this at the time, but she mentioned it to me much later.

Dean suggested that we catch a cab home, and I hesitated. In my head, I began excusing all of his faults to justify going home with him. I put his drinking down to first-day nerves. Part of me was just desperate for a boyfriend, having been single for a long time. I found him attractive, and I suspect that my hormones played a big role in me ignoring the warning signs. As full as my life has been, I have often felt lonely, and I did not want to miss out on a chance at love. I left my friends and we headed to Dean's place.

When we arrived, I looked around in surprise. It looked a bit like a grandmother's home with ornate furniture and old ornaments scattered around. It was then that he explained he was renting a room in a house with an older woman who he didn't really get on with very well. I found it very odd that a forty-year-old man would rent a room in a house with someone he didn't connect with, but once again, I ignored this warning sign.

We became intimate that night and he was not able to function very well because he was so drunk. He ended up falling asleep on me and I couldn't wake him up. This was quite irritating but not surprising, and I decided to leave. I left a note and snuck out, reached a main road, and flagged down a taxi to return to the hotel. I was kind of relieved that I had escaped and was thinking that I probably wouldn't see him again.

Around 5 a.m., the phone rang in my hotel room. It was Dean, who had woken up and realised that I had gone. He was seriously apologetic and wanted to make it up to me by cooking dinner for me the next day. I allowed him to convince me, despite the nagging doubt in the pit of my stomach.

I wish I had known how important it is to trust your instincts and not to ignore red flags. Listen to your gut in these situations, because more often than not, your instincts will be correct. I am disappointed in how little I had learned with regard to this lesson over the years of mistakes that I've made with men. Sometimes I would like to slap my younger self to shake me out of my hormone-driven stupor.

I agreed to meet him again, went back to his flat and he cooked me a steak with vegetables. The woman he shared a house with was not home, so we ate in the lounge room, and I was able to take my time looking around at the strange mix of garish and kitsch décor that filled this woman's oddly furnished home. Dean told me a lot about how successful his business was, and we had a good laugh and got on well. We spent the night together and it was lovely, and I wondered if I had misjudged him. I decided to see him again after the girls and I returned from a few days in Las Vegas and San Francisco.

At some point, I discovered that Dean was fifty-three, not forty as he had told me. I remember driving with him and my friends and he was telling us about the many accomplishments he had achieved in his life and I joked with him, saying, 'Are you sure you're only forty? You would have to be much older to have done all of that.' Little did I know, he was lying to me about his age, amongst other things.

I went with the girls to Las Vegas and we were having a great time. Dean kept calling me and wanted to come and meet us in San Francisco after Vegas. I said that was fine, and he said he would book a flight. He called back later to say his credit card wasn't working and asked if he could use mine. In my typical naïve, generous fashion, I agreed to let him. I gave him my card details for the website he was booking flights on. He promised to pay me back.

I am sure people were already being scammed in the relatively young world of online dating, but I had not heard of this type of behaviour. I was so fixated on my search for love that I ignored the signs that Dean might be after my money. It did, however, occur to my girlfriends that he was dodgy, but I brushed off their warnings. They were getting increasingly worried and decided they did not like this guy at all.

Dean met us in San Francisco and things got weird as he would grab a drink at any opportunity. I could tell that my friends were starting to think he was a bit of an idiot. I also seemed to be paying for lots for things because his card was mysteriously not working in the ATM and he could not get money out of the bank. One night, we went out for sushi, and when it came time to pay the bill, he mysteriously disappeared. I paid for him and he did not offer to pay me back.

When it came time for us to leave San Francisco and for Dean to return to LA, he asked us to drive him to the airport. I was up for it, but one of my mates put her foot down and said, 'no way'. It was not on our route out of town and she was really sick of him taking advantage of me and did not want to go out of her way to help him. I gave him money for a taxi so he could get to the airport.

It was a relief to just travel with the girls once again and it was nice not to have to worry about Dean and his drinking or lack of cash, but despite that, when I got back to LA, I decided that I would not go to Atlanta with the girls but would stay with Dean. The girls were disappointed that I was not going with them but were still hopeful that something positive would come out of my connection with Dean, although from their perspective, things were not looking too good.

Dean and I decided to go to Santa Barbara for a couple of nights in a car I hired (he claimed he owned a car, but it was at the mechanics). Dean also said that he could not find his driver's licence, so only I could drive the car, as he was not able to be covered by the insurance. I later came to suspect that he had most likely lost his licence for drunk driving as it was becoming clear that he was quite a heavy drinker with very little self-control.

I disliked the way that he interacted with hotel staff in Santa Barbara, and the way he spoke to his clients on the phone also troubled me because he was just arrogant and volatile when speaking to others. He was verbally abusive, self-righteous, and obnoxious. It was dawning on me that I did not want to stay with this guy. However, every time I was about to voice my concerns or extricate myself from the situation, it was like he had a sixth sense and he would go on a charm offensive to reel me back in.

I must confess, these tactics worked. I kept second-guessing myself, and looking back, I realise I was being gaslighted by him, just like Goran had done when I was married and pregnant so many years ago. Dean's way of gaslighting me was to lie to me, wear me down, and throw in positive reinforcement to confuse me, although his actions did not match his words. True to form, I ignored my gut instincts, made excuses for him in my head, and let his compliments and flattery push my concerns to the back of my mind.

One night, he disappeared from the hotel room. I went downstairs to the car park and realised the car was gone. I was furious. Old feelings associated with my ex-boyfriend Stan when he ran off with my car came flooding back. I felt betrayed and frustrated that he would take it upon himself to drive off in the car, without asking and without a licence, while I was asleep. I had a feeling Dean would be at the local bar down the road, so I got dressed and walked down there. Just as I suspected, there was the car, and Dean was inside drinking with an older woman. I was livid and demanded the car keys. He gave them to me and then followed me out apologising profusely and begging me to let him come back to the hotel. He promised me it would not happen again, he said that he didn't mean to take the car or to upset me, and he showered me with compliments. I fell for his words rather than focusing on his actions.

The next morning, I woke up feeling sick with nerves over my situation. I went outside to have a cry in the car. I kept re-living the night before and realised that I had not dealt with it well and that perhaps I had missed my chance to get away from him. I called the airline from the car to change my flight back to Hong Kong and then I went back inside to pack my bags. I made Dean get up and told him we were leaving. He packed in a stupor, as he had a hangover, and I made him pay for the hotel on his credit card. Miraculously, the card now seemed to work, and he paid for the room. We drove back to LA in a cloud of tension.

On the way back to LA, I told him that I didn't trust him and was going home to Hong Kong. He begged me for another chance, and at one point I stopped the car and burst into tears as the stress and emotional pressure of the whole trip were getting to me. The internal battle that I was having with myself was doing my head in. By the time we arrived back in LA, he had convinced me to stay and I changed my flights back again so I could stay a few more days.

The first night back in LA he left me in his room and disappeared all night with my hire car. I felt sick being left alone locked in the room in his strange and unwelcoming share house. At one point, his roommate knocked on the door wanting to have the phone that was in his room, but I didn't know if she knew I was there, so I didn't know what to do. I just sat there hoping he would get home soon so he could give her the phone. I could not believe that after all his efforts to get me to stay longer, he would leave me alone all night.

He returned in the morning and said he had been with a friend who was upset and needed his support. Once again, I fell for his excuses and let go of my disappointment at being left alone.

I am embarrassed by my level of naïveté and the fact that I kept taking this terrible treatment like I deserved it. In hindsight, I can see he was an expert at manipulation and my self-esteem and conviction were not strong enough for me to take action or make a stand against his behaviour.

Dean said that the woman he shared a house with did not want me to stay there, so I booked a hotel at Venice Beach and he stayed with me. We went shopping and he convinced me to buy him an expensive bracelet. In retrospect, I think a large part of me believed that I could buy affection, or if I was generous to others, then they would respect or love me more.

We went out to a local bar, and once again, he got so drunk that he could barely walk home. He staggered along the beach and fell into the water. It was a nightmare to get him back to the hotel. I realised that I had made a massive mistake again and that this guy was a loser. I will never forget the sick feeling that I had in my stomach. It was a combination of fear, shame, nervousness, and embarrassment.

Luckily, I was due to fly home the next day, so I was able to leave him without a confrontation and I figured that I would never even talk to him again. As I was boarding at LAX, Dean called and asked for my address in Hong Kong so he could send a gift. I gave it to him and thought that maybe he wasn't so bad after all.

Once I was back in Hong Kong, I happened to be looking at my credit card statement and saw that it had been used to pay bills in the USA while I was on the flight back to Hong Kong. He had not intended to send me a gift. He used my address to pay his bills with my credit card as clearly he had kept the number when he bought the flight to San Francisco. I guess, being such an honest person, it never occurred to me that someone could be so calculating and fraudulent.

I called Dean and threatened to contact the police if he did not return my money, and I said I had proof I was on a flight while the transactions were being made and that he was committing fraud and could be charged. My threat worked and he paid me back the money he had stolen. I cancelled my credit card and ordered a new one. I never heard from Dean again.

This was just the beginning. I wish it wasn't true, but subsequent decisions show that it took me years before these life lessons began to take hold. I feel embarrassed and vulnerable whenever I recount stories from this part of my life, but I know now it would take a long time and some deeply frightening lessons before I could really, truly 'get it'. If just one person can learn from my mistakes, then my efforts here will be worthwhile.

A Glimpse of Hope

When my daughter left home and went to university, my loneliness intensified. It had always been just the two of us for most of her life, so when she was not around anymore, my single life was a constant reminder that I was alone and did not have someone to share my life with. My ex-husband used to tell me that I lived in a 'Brady Bunch' world, and maybe there was some truth to this claim. I think part of me wanted a wholesome family life. I was certainly an idealist; I came from a very stable, loving family home where my parents loved each other and are still happily married.

Hong Kong is a notoriously difficult place to meet a partner due to the fast-paced lifestyle, long working hours, and small number of expats. Despite the problems I faced meeting Dean in the USA, I soldiered on with my efforts at online dating. One guy was called Wilson, and his profile handle was Evol ('Love' backwards). He didn't want to talk on the phone and preferred to chat by email or text, but eventually I got him on the line. He was from Africa; I can't remember where, but maybe it was Senegal, as he had a French accent. I had been getting cold feet about going to meet him as the emotional connection was not great over text and email, but I felt better once we had spoken.

After a few months of communicating with him, I caught a ferry from Hong Kong to Jiangmen in China, where he lived. When I arrived, he was the same as his pictures (albeit older and skinnier) and seemed to be who he said he was except for one fact: I had told him that I was an atheist, and he had claimed that he was not religious. Now that I was there, he was kneeling by the side of his bed to pray and talking to me about his Christian beliefs and his belief in intelligent design. This made me want to run a mile, as I simply do not share those values. He was a nice guy and was interesting and kind, but he was not for me. He took this information in his stride and I left early to come back to Hong Kong.

My next adventure was with Trevor, who was from the USA and was working in Shanghai. He seemed straightforward, honest, and nice. We chatted online for a few months and we spoke face to face on Skype. He invited me to visit him for a few days during one of my holidays.

We had a great time and I got to see Shanghai for the first time. It was exciting to see this beautiful waterfront metropolis in China. We wandered around the markets, and it was terrific to experience this bustling city full of busy people and historical buildings. I stayed in his spare room and we got on well.

Trevor was a very calm and friendly guy who treated me with respect. He was tall and handsome with an air of maturity and kindness about him that was very attractive. We had a nice time together and he was just like he was when we were chatting before I met him. However, it was evident to me that there was not a romantic connection from his side and I know that I ruined things by smoking. I could tell that he hated it and did not want to date a smoker.

Next, I met a guy called Dave from Kenya, an engineer living in Osaka, Japan. We emailed, Skyped, and texted and got to know each other. I eventually agreed to go and visit him in Japan during one of my holidays.

When I got there, once again, it felt a bit awkward. I was staying with him in his room. I hadn't checked to see if he had a spare room before I agreed to stay with him and there was only one bedroom. He offered to sleep on the couch and give me the room, which was nice of him. He made me feel welcome and appeared to be genuine. He showed me his workplace, I met some of the people he worked with, we went to a beach party and I met his friends. The problem was that I was not attracted to him. He understood and respected my choice not to become romantically involved with him. I left him after about a four-day visit and felt like I had made a new friend. I know that he was much keener on me than I was on him, and he wished something more could develop. We stayed in touch for a while after my visit, but eventually we lost contact.

Given these last three experiences, I felt that dating someone from the internet might actually work. Each of these men were kind, decent and treated me respectfully. I am definitely a cup-half-full kind of gal. After the disaster that was Dean, it was great to meet men who were interesting, and all would have made great partners for the right woman. It was validating to meet people who were true to how they presented themselves online. I expected nothing less the next time I met someone online and hoped to build a relationship with someone special.

Hope Springs Eternal

One day in late 2008, I was looking at online dating sites and saw an incredibly handsome guy who was in Hong Kong. Wow, finally someone who was actually in my city! I messaged him and we got chatting and decided that we would meet up for a drink in Lan Kwai Fong, the bar district in Hong Kong.

I first saw him waiting under a lamp post in Lan Kwai Fong. I found him so instantly physically appealing that my heart skipped a beat. We went for a drink and he became even more attractive, as he was funny, engaging, and seemed like a lovely man. His name was Gary, and he was a few years younger than me. He said he was an exporter and importer from Nigeria.

We dated for a couple of months, and as we became closer, our feelings for each other grew stronger. One day, he said that he was getting kicked out of his room in his flat in Kowloon, the area across the harbour from Central, Hong Kong. I offered for him to come and stay with me and see how it went. He was excited at the prospect of living with me, and he moved into my house. He didn't have many belongings and came over with a few bags of clothes.

It was like having a real boyfriend for the first time in years. We went to my friend's wedding, hung out with my mates, and had a really great time. He was calm, kind, and very handsome. We began talking about going on holiday abroad. On the surface, I was happy, but there was something troubling me in the pit of my stomach.

One day, we were coming home to the island from Hong Kong on a ferry. Gary seemed stressed and worried. I kept asking him what was wrong, but he clearly did not want to tell me. This made me feel quite nervous, and I wondered what was going on. My gut told me it was something significant.

Finally, at my insistence, Gary told me that he had not been completely honest with me. He was an illegal immigrant in Hong Kong and did not have a passport. This information floored me. I could not believe that he kept this from me. He realised that he had to tell me because he could not leave the country for our holiday. Of course, this also meant that he could not get a job. He had been living on the very little money he made sending things like mobile phones back to Nigeria and other minor jobs that he did not go into detail about. I also discovered that his name was actually Benny Gary and that he used both names depending on which name suited his circumstances. He had also lied to me about his age and was a couple of years younger than he had claimed.

We talked through different possible scenarios to solve this issue, but this was not a good situation for us to be in. I did not want to be dating an illegal immigrant who did not even have a passport. He was suggesting ways that he could get a passport on the black market, and that just made me even more certain that I had to get out of this situation.

However, I was torn. I had strong feelings for him, and apart from this disaster, everything else was going well. My daughter was away at university but had met him once, she was happy for me and hopeful that it would work out. She may have been dubious, as she had learned to be wary of the men I dated given my chequered past, but she said she was supportive, and I hated to disappoint her. Part of me was also afraid to say goodbye to what we had built, even though deep down, I knew that's what I had to do.

Not long after this revelation, I got home before Gary and went on my laptop to check my emails. He had left his email account open, and to my horror, there were about twenty emails to another woman in Hong Kong, professing his love to her. I could not believe it. My heart was pounding out of my chest as

I read all of these emails. This was obviously a Chinese woman he was dating in Hong Kong. He was telling her that he was in mainland China working to save money for their future. He was in love with her, missed her, and would come and see her soon. I was running a school trip overseas in the coming weeks, and that is when he told her that he was returning from China and he couldn't wait to see her.

I was furious, but at the same time, relieved. This was the excuse to break up with him I had been looking for, as I did not want to be with someone who was illegally in the country. However, I was still significantly hurt and shocked at the deception and the realisation that he was regularly writing emails to her while living with me. I felt sick, angry, and deceived—feelings that were beginning to seem all too familiar.

I packed all of his stuff in bags and put it in the front garden. There were so many clothes that I had bought him and I resisted the urge to chop them into shreds. The thought crossed my mind, but that is not really my style. I texted him and told him that I had seen all of his emails to his girlfriend and that he could get out of my house immediately. He came home within an hour of receiving the text, stood forlornly at the front door and knocked. I opened the door just a fraction and asked him to give me back my house key and he handed it to me. I said goodbye calmly and shut the door in his face. He then sat on a seat in the front garden and started to cry. He pleaded with me to forgive him and made all sorts of promises, but there was not a chance. Eventually, he took all of his things and left.

I contacted this woman by email to let her know that we were both being duped by this guy. She was very appreciative of the email and was clearly upset. She emailed me back a week or so later to say that she had ended her relationship with him as well. She said that she had felt that something was wrong and didn't really believe all that he was telling her about living in mainland China. So, in the end, he lost both of us.

About a year later, I saw him in Lan Kwai Fong with a young blonde woman. They were walking hand in hand into a bar and sat down for a drink. I took a deep breath and walked up to them. When Gary first saw me, a big smile spread across his face and he was about to be affable, like I was a long-lost old friend. However, I stopped him in his tracks and warned the girl to be careful because he was a duplicitous liar. I then said goodbye and walked out. I didn't want the same thing to happen to her that had happened to me. I never saw him again.

The Addict in Shenzhen

For some reason, I am dreading telling this part of my story and have even considered leaving it out. I guess I feel a lot of shame around this brief relationship and regret getting involved at all. Once again, it cost me money and I was duped. Remember that pattern?

I met this guy Tyrone while online dating; he lived just over the border in China in a city called Shenzhen. This was quite exciting for me, as Shenzhen is only a one-hour train ride from Hong Kong, and as an Aussie, I can easily get a visa at the border. It seemed possible that this might be someone whom I could see on a more regular basis.

Tyrone was from the USA, and I had that same old sinking feeling in the pit of my stomach when I saw his email handle, 'Tyrone Moneyman,' but I ignored this gnawing ache of concern. We started chatting and began Skyping for a while. He was a school teacher in Shenzhen and had been living there for five years. He lived at the school, which I thought seemed a bit odd, but I didn't give it too much thought.

We talked through Skype, although the video connection was not great, and sometimes I thought I could see that something was wrong with his teeth. Other than that, he was handsome, fun, and seemed like a nice guy. He was around my age and taller than me. I felt that someone raised in the USA would have a cultural upbringing somewhat closer to mine and that this could make it easier to connect.

At some point, Tyrone mentioned that he had left the USA to escape a drug addiction. He said he was five years sober and that leaving the USA was the best thing that he had ever done. I am not sure why I didn't end things then and there because this revelation was a massive red flag. I like to try and find the good in people, and for better or worse I generally want to believe people are being truthful. I try not to be judgmental because I do think anyone can overcome past mistakes and be a better person for it. I decided I would explore things a bit further with him to see how it would go.

He agreed to visit me in Hong Kong and we would meet at the IFC, a big shopping centre in Central close to the ferry pier. The first time we met, he was walking towards me and I couldn't believe how old he looked. He was hunched over and shuffling along like a very old man, yet he was only a year or two older than me. Once we began talking, I was shocked to see that he was missing his front teeth. A million panicked thoughts ran through my head in quick succession. I wondered why his teeth were missing. Was it related to drug use? Why would he not have them fixed? How could he teach like this? Was this a deal-breaker for me? However, we had made enough of a connection on Skype that I was not willing to let it go over something that could be easily fixed.

The first time he came to my house, he went upstairs to look at the view. Then he came downstairs and told me how happy he was to have met me, and that standing upstairs looking out at the beautiful island in front of him, he felt nostalgic and content because he had finally 'made it' in life by meeting me. I thought this was a really odd thing to say, and once again, ignored that weird feeling in my stomach. I took it as a sign that he was looking for someone successful, and felt he had found that in me.

We spent all of our time together at my place. I was too embarrassed to take him out in public because I did not want my friends to see his missing front teeth. Even though I could accept it as they could be fixed quickly, I felt that my friends would judge him and me in the process, and I wanted to avoid that at all costs.

I arranged an appointment with my dentist, and the next time Tyrone came to visit, he received new teeth, at my expense.

He said he was going to pay me back, but of course, never did. Once he had new teeth, he looked great, and we were able to go out and mix with my friends. He was funny, charming and they seemed to like him. Finally, I felt like all was right with the world and that we might have a chance to develop something between us.

One day, Tyrone was working in his school in Shenzhen and I had a day off for some reason. It was in between his lessons and we were chatting on Skype. Suddenly, Tyrone picked up a longneck beer bottle that was sitting just out of my view and took a swig from it while he was talking to me. I couldn't believe my eyes, so I challenged him and asked him if he was drinking on the job, while teaching children. I was horrified.

He was shocked and had obviously accidentally taken a swig of the beer in front of me and had to admit that he was drinking on the job. I couldn't fathom that anyone responsible for teaching children could be so reckless. Then I thought back to other times when we had been Skyping when I could see boxes of empty beer bottles behind him, and when I asked him about it, he claimed they were his friends' bottles left during visits. I also remembered the times when he was drinking out of a coffee mug while we were Skyping at night and he would become increasingly animated and louder. I didn't realise that perhaps he was drinking alcohol and pretending it was coffee.

I recalled coming home during one of his visits to find him passed out on my sofa and finding a vodka bottle and beer bottles hidden in my bin. He had only been at the house for a few hours. Once again, I am embarrassed to say that I pushed all of these negative signs out of my mind. However, when I realised he was drinking at work and was drunk on the job working with children, that crossed a line. I told him I was done. He begged me for another chance, but I said no way. He was clearly an alcoholic but was trying his best to hide it from me. Once again, I had been betrayed by a man. I tried to get the money he owed me for his teeth, but I never received a cent back. I never saw him again, either.

My One 'Tru' Man

Scammed Big Time

I was in Hong Kong Skyping with a friend in Australia who told me she had met this awesome guy on a new dating site. He was in the UK, and she felt like she was really developing a relationship with him. I decided to check out the dating site, as my old ones were clearly not working for me.

I saw this profile:

Name: Truman
Age: 35
Lives: Manchester, United Kingdom
Occupation: Construction / Trades

I indicated my interest, and he replied with a message about himself. It was most likely a generic reply that he sent to everyone, but I did not even consider this at the time. I thought he was writing this directly to me from his heart.

Thank you for all your interests, favourites, and messages. I wish you all luck finding love, but please remember the words of Ms Marilyn Monroe... 'I'm selfish, impatient, and a little insecure. I make mistakes, I am out of control and at times hard to handle. But if you can't handle me at my worst, then you sure as hell don't deserve me at my best!' Okay, a bit about me... I am a tall, prosperous, kindly professional. I am a director of a property/project management/construction company. I'm self-motivating, intuitive, with varied interests and people-orientated. My likes are building, conversation, golf, theatre, books, travel, wining and dining. Dislikes are pomposity, personal violence, and women who believe that true virtue is located below the navel. I am funny, with a high IQ and income. I have a sparkling, confident smile, shiny brown skin, a trimmed moustache, rich brown eyes, and shaved bald head. I am looking for a sexy lady to share travel and excitement, maybe more. So this is unlikely to suit pushy materialists. Should this meet the eye of a loving, nice lady who enjoys concerts, movies, quiet times, and finer things in life, why not contact me and tell me about yourself? No photo, no chat, sorry. If it hasn't happened to you yet, it could with this optimistic, talented, and charming man. Thank you for reading my profile.

It's obvious now that he was writing to many women, not just one. I did not see that at the time. Crikey, how naïve and gullible I was, again! It makes me feel sad for the person I was back then.

He seemed like a great guy from his message, and I wrote to him. This was my first message:

You seem very interesting and genuine. I like your pictures as well, you have a great smile! I am an Aussie girl living in Hong Kong. I am six feet tall, long dark hair, and very active. I play different sports and love to swim. I am a teacher at an international school and I teach drama and personal, social, and health education. I am also a Head of Year so I look after the students' academic needs and emotional, social problems as well. I love my job, so I am really lucky.

I live on a little island off Hong Kong which is a Chinese fishing village with great beaches. There are no cars and I walk everywhere. I travel loads; actually, I have just returned from Kenya with 60 students on a school trip, which was amazing.

I have a daughter who is a beautiful, successful girl. She is 21 and she lives in London. Do you travel much, and have you been anywhere in Asia? Do you have any children?

Anyway, have a great day and let me know if you would like to learn more about me. I hope to hear back from you.

Cheers,
Jules

This is the first reply I received from Truman in November 2010:

It was really nice to hear from you. I have been wondering when a Joan of Arc with substance and looks to match would come along... I hope your love trip online is going well. Not so for me, it's all been fake profiles, demands for money or phone credit, scams, etc. I am left wondering where all the good ladies in the world are. I am so thrilled about the concept of living on an island with no cars... how unbelievably cool. You sound quite happy and good on you. Life is short and you seem to have got it right... simple is better! I am planning my trip back in time soon. The Gambia, Ghana, Kenya are all on my planned travel route. I am at work, but decided to reply to you quickly... Until our energy attracts again.

Take care,
Truman

It is very interesting that Truman, the would-be scammer, commented on being scammed himself on the dating site. This was great psychology to use to put my mind at ease. It made me think that he was a genuine guy.

My reply was:

Hi Truman,

Wow, thanks for the awesome email. Nice to hear from you, too! It's interesting that you ask about my experience on this site. I have only been on a few weeks and have received hundreds of messages and interests... a ridiculous amount, 99% of which I have deleted. I have chatted to one guy in Sweden who was very nice but too young; apart from that, you're the second one. I have been burnt before with internet dating and have some interesting stories to tell but not much luck, I must say.

There certainly are people out there whose intentions are neither honourable nor straight up. We live and learn and I never give up hope for a decent, honest, loving partner to share my life with. There are some fantastic people out in the world; they just seem to be few and far between on the internet.

As a six-foot woman in Hong Kong, as you can imagine, I struggle to meet men. Thus, the internet seems to be my only hope. I can't leave this wonderful lifestyle and job that I have in search of love because there are no guarantees anywhere. Anyway, rest assured, I am genuine and only looking for love and a partner to share all the great things in life there are to be enjoyed. I really want to travel with someone, through Africa and South America. I would love to do a couple of months in each place, which is possible given I am a teacher and we get long summer holidays.

I love Africa and have a strong affinity for it. I have been to Kenya five times with over 260 kids in total. They have been life-changing trips for many of my students and they appreciate what they have so much more and care more about others. It's quite rewarding, and we make a huge difference to kids along the way in Kenya. We took 300 pairs of trainers to a school in Barringo; it was brilliant, as every kid got a pair of shoes in the school and the joy over a simple pair of shoes was not lost on my students who have everything and more. Priceless!
I have also been to Madagascar, where I pulled out some of my high school French and surprised myself with what I remembered. I have been to South Africa twice, Egypt, and I think that's it so far. Oh, Mauritius too.

I come from Adelaide in Australia and I grew up on a farm and went to boarding school, which I loved. I came to Hong Kong 10 years ago when my daughter was 11. I put her through university on my own and now she is working in London. I play netball and am in the top division 1 team in Hong Kong, although my ankles are telling me I should retire but the rest of me won't let me. I also love to swim and scuba dive. I play beach volleyball, although lately we have been playing pétanque (boules) and commenting on how we are not as active as we used to be. I have loads of friends here on my little island from all over the world. We are an eclectic bunch... bit of a dysfunctional family one might say, but we have an amazing life here, as there is never a dull moment.

I have just finished working 19 days straight (with the Kenya trip in the middle) and am thrilled that it is the weekend. I look forward to hearing more about you and your life. Please ask me anything you would like to know about me.

Thanks for inspiring me to share so much with you. I enjoyed your message!

Take care and I hope to hear from you soon.

Later... I hope,
Jules

After that, we decided to share Skype addresses and began messaging each other.

Falling for His Lies

So, our relationship began. We wrote on Skype and also chatted on the phone a few times. I thought his accent was a bit odd and questioned him about it. He told me that he was born in the UK and was adopted by a British couple. He said that his parents sent him to Canada for boarding school and that explained his unusual accent. In hindsight, I realise that he was just talking rubbish and his accent was not British with a little Canadian twang, but his story threw me off and convinced me to trust him.

Early on, Truman's Skype name changed to Truman Buharay and it did not match his name, which he told me was Truman Buhari. I did not notice this at the time, but I questioned him sometime later, and he brushed me off. When I asked what his job was, he replied that he was a project and business development manager for a successful property company—'full throttle, baby', as he put it.

On the phone, he said he would like to visit me in Hong Kong, to which I said he could. However, soon after, he made an excuse about work and said he couldn't come to see me and asked if perhaps I could visit him or suggested we meet in Africa for a holiday. I cannot believe I was considering going to meet him in Ghana for a holiday, having never even met him in person. That was absolute madness, and thank goodness it never happened.

Given that sending pictures was his condition for initiating our relationship, I sent him some photos of the island I live on and of me. He began getting sappy, and I rose to the occasion and joined him with sentimental rhetoric.

Truman: Keep them coming...
Truman: Your mails cheer me up...
Jules: Will do.
Truman: Your photo is on my computer background.
Truman: It's a battle between your picture and the island.
Truman: I do not know which I love more. Lol.
Truman: I stare at you all day...
Jules: I want you to love us both equally, me and my island. Lol.
Truman: Difficult one...
Truman: The island photo going on tomorrow. Lol.
Jules: Nice.
Jules: You can interchange them.
Truman: I do...

Positively sickening! I want people to see how men like this, preying on loneliness and goodwill, can suck some people into thinking they're really interested, when they're actually professional scammers. We had been speaking on the phone a lot as well, so he was working me from two different angles. I asked for some of his pictures, which he initially ignored. After quite a while, he finally sent some photos.

In these chat logs, you will notice that some lines of conversation seem to overlap. This is because we are typing too fast to keep up with each other.

Jules: Did you like the photos I sent?
Truman: I do...
Jules: Can you please send me some photos of you? I don't have any.
Truman: You are a sexy lady...
Jules: Thanks, glad you think so.
Jules: I was wondering how someone as hot as you can be single in a place like the UK?
Truman: They're just not my kind of women...
Truman: I just came out of a long relationship.
Truman: I just want a simple, nice woman.
Truman: Not spoilt, unrealistic, and selfish.

Jules: I don't know if any women are simple... I think we can be a bit complicated.
Truman: I try to always look for good in people.
Jules: Oh yeah, I am not any of those.
Truman: One of my many faults...
Jules: My faults are being too trusting, too naïve, and too generous.

Little did I know this last line would have been music to his ears, exactly what he was really looking for in a woman. Without realising it, I had made it clear to him that I was an easy target. I was a scammer's dream come true.

Truman (an ironic name, as he was not a true man at all!) went on to tell me about his career, which of course I later found out was all lies as well. He claimed to have a degree in project management, and was responsible for three projects each worth £2 million. He continued to boast about himself, then used my interests to reel me in a little more, and I fell hook, line, and sinker.

Truman: They say I am the best...
Truman: If Tru can't do it, it can't be done.
Jules: I am sure you're brilliant.
Jules: In an ideal world what would you like to be doing for a job?
Truman: Working with children.
Truman: I love kids.
Truman: Helping the less fortunate in Africa.
Jules: Yeah, that's our plan, you and me in Africa saving lives and making a difference.
Jules: We can work towards that.
Truman: I already am...
Jules: Anything is possible, you know?
Truman: I am going to buy land and build a home for orphans.
Jules: We could be an amazing team.
Truman: Motherless babies and babies with HIV.
Jules: Fantastic! Count me in.
Truman: I am going to take care of them myself... all the way through to university.

Truman: Can you imagine that?

Jules: Wow! I have the same aspirations!

Jules: Yes, totally!

Truman: Having tons of kids owe their life and future to us...

Jules: I so hope we click on all levels, fall in love, and can make this happen.

Truman: That's why I am working so hard.

Jules: A new and exciting chapter in our lives.

Truman: Because I know there is a life in Africa I am going to save.

Jules: Good for you. I am ready when you are.

Truman: We need to go do our homework.

Jules: We just have to decide where?

Truman: Maybe go to Africa for 7 days?

Truman: 29th Jan?

Jules: We will chat face to face on Skype this weekend and make a plan.

Truman: I would love to go with you...

Jules: Me too. I will go anywhere that we can be safe to do our work.

Truman: We can brainstorm this weekend.

Jules: We will. It will be amazing. Do you have any sense of where you come from?

Truman: I will always protect you.

Truman: I have a black belt in judo.

Jules: I know you will. This is so amazing that we have met. Your dream has been my dream also but I wanted to do it with my partner.

Jules: Very exciting. I feel intuitively very calm and sure that we were made for each other.

Truman: I don't know why, I feel it too...

Jules: I have been looking and waiting for you for a long time.

Truman: Have you ever been in love before?

Jules: I have been in love twice in my 20s but not since, really. The thing is, I don't think that I have ever truly had someone who loves me.

Jules: You?

Truman: I just hope we don't let each other down when we meet!

Jules: I don't think we will. All the chips are falling nicely into place so far.

Truman: I wasted 14 years on a woman that didn't know the meaning of love...
Jules: We will increase the connection when we talk face to face. We will be ok.
Jules: Nothing is a waste because it all shapes who you are today.
Jules: I have been single for most of the last 14 years, so I have been without love for ages.
Jules: It's ok because good things come to those who wait and I have been waiting for you.
Jules: We have so much to look forward to.
Jules: I wish you could come to Hong Kong over Christmas break. I would have come to you if my daughter and her boyfriend weren't coming here.
Jules: Even though it's freezing in your neck of the woods.
Truman: I am so sleepy...
Jules: Go to bed, babe.

He had me going a mile a minute, and I was quick to let him leave at the slightest hint that he was done. It is so interesting to read this now because it is right out of the scammer's handbook, but I was completely oblivious to any of it at the time. I was just enamoured with his desire to be with me and have a relationship. Everything I had always wanted suddenly felt possible.

He was increasing my connection with him by appearing to share the same dreams as me. He knew that I had taken students to Kenya and was drawing from my history and love of helping kids with the fantasy of going to Africa together. By opening up with all his talk about how good he was at his job, how big the projects were, and how much money was involved in them, he seemed accomplished, successful, and important, allowing me to believe that 'our' dreams could come true.

He was very good at avoiding topics that he did not want to discuss. He avoided the question about where his ancestors might have been from originally, and when I suggested he come and see me in Hong Kong, he shut that down by saying he was sleepy.

As I think back on how it all began, I realise that we can have great wisdom with hindsight, but to be honest, I really overlooked so much that I should not have. I was trusting and took him at face value.

Lies, Damn Lies

Truman worked hard to convince me he had two careers running alongside each other. I did not consider at the time that he was supposedly a senior project manager in a multimillion-dollar construction company. If this was the case, how could he have had the time to run and work in a mobile phone shop on the side—and why would he? I cannot understand why I did not question this at all. It did not cross my mind. I just thought he was such an incredibly hard worker. Oh, my stars!

We always messaged each other in our Skype conversations as he said his web cam was broken. He never Skyped with me face to face. When I asked him to, he said I needed to teach him how to set it up. What kind of person owns a phone shop and can 'sell, fix, unlock phones, and find parts and accessories,' as he described to me, and cannot manage to video chat?

Instead, we continued to make plans to meet in person. At first we were going to meet in Ghana, but then he said he couldn't leave his phone business so he couldn't make it to Africa. He said he would love to come and see me in Hong Kong, but both his jobs prevented him from doing it at that time, so he asked if I could come to him. I had two weeks of holidays coming up, so I decided I would go to see him in Manchester for a week after my daughter and her boyfriend returned from their visit to Hong Kong.

I accepted his friend request on Facebook, and noticed that he didn't have many friends. One of them was a pretty blonde girl from Sweden. He later mentioned her and said that she had refused to visit him and that annoyed him, so he ended it with her—a little early intimidation to remind me to be loyal and generous.

Here is what I wrote when I had booked my ticket to see him. He didn't answer as he probably couldn't believe his luck and was possibly in shock.

Jules: Hey there, I have a flight booked on the 26th December arriving on 27th (will let you know time as can't remember) then I fly out on the evening of the 1st Jan (I might leave a bit earlier in the day and meet my daughter in London for a bit... I will see). I will just send the ticket to you later. Does that all sound ok with you? I am very excited. Please get a new web cam so we can Skype this weekend and see each other. I am off to bed now. Hope I can sleep in my excited state. Catch you soon.

Most scammers do not meet their intended victims. They groom them over time to make them think they are in love from afar and then they start to try and get money from them. I often wonder if Truman was angling for money from me for a ticket to Ghana, but his plan was foiled by me flying to see him in the UK. That may have thrown a spanner in the works and hence the radio silence when I told him I bought a ticket.

The next time we spoke, he told me I had a 'beautiful smile and lovely honest eyes' and we had some random chit-chat about my netball and my visit to see him. I also had to ask him again—for the third time—to get a web cam.

Jules: So are you ok if I visit from 27th December to 1st January, or is that too long?
Truman: I would love you to come and spend those days and New Year's with me.
Jules: Great, that's fabulous. I will send you flight details.
Truman: I am going to book us a nice treat.
Jules: Oh lovely, I am really excited you know. It's going to be fabulous.

Truman: I really do care about you...
Truman: And feel very excited too...
Truman: I hope we make it.
Jules: Please can you get a web cam so we can build on that connection before I come?
Jules: Love is very elusive.
Truman: I know...
Truman: I have had it before and it's the most beautiful thing in the world.
Truman: I respect you so much...
Jules: We're on the same page which is amazing. We both want a deep and meaningful relationship with true love.
Jules: You're lucky! I hope we can have it, too.
Truman: What you did with your daughter, moving to Hong Kong and making it there...
Truman: You are a strong woman.
Truman: I just want to know I have someone who cares about me out there...
Truman: Who loves me for me.
Jules: She wants me to be happy.
Jules: She is sick of seeing me make bad choices and getting hurt.
Jules: She wants me to meet a decent man who thinks I am amazing.
Truman: Good. I am that man.
Truman: I was in a 14-year relationship. I was so good to her. I stood by her. For her to forsake me...
Jules: Yes, the 14 years shows you can be loyal and committed.
Truman: I am getting all emotional...
Truman: I need a time out.
Jules: Don't be sad.
Truman: Take care, my love...
Jules: Things happen for a reason.
Truman: No... I am happy that I may have found my soul mate and God has answered my prayers.

Blimey, he's good, sucking me in with his emotional 'I've been hurt before' rhetoric. Reading this back was quite cathartic; I can see how he fooled me and how I fell for his fake platitudes. I feel a little less angry, and instead I feel sorry for myself for being conned by this smooth-talking charlatan. At least I can now see that he was very good at scamming me with his words.

In one of our previous phone conversations, he told me we were going to spend a weekend at a posh spa hotel, hence the 'nice treat' he was going to book. I researched the venue and it looked gorgeous and very expensive. He was going to pay for the whole weekend as a thank you for me paying to come and see him. Oh, how sweet, I thought. I was excited to be taken care of, for a change.

It's also interesting to note that this was the second time he told me about being in a previous relationship and I fell right into his trap by confirming what he wanted me to believe from that claim: that he was loyal and committed.

You can see my excitement at going to meet him in this exchange below. Sadly, my naïveté is also evident in this passage and is an indicator that I was thinking with my heart and not my brain.

Jules: I have paid for my ticket so operation Tru and Jules connection is under way!
Jules: I also bought some warm clothes for the trip.
Truman: How much was it, babes?
Jules: The clothes cost more than the flight!
Jules: Just kidding.
Truman: Lol.
Jules: I am excited!
Truman: I have a doctor's appointment...
Jules: Can you buy a web cam? We could Skype when you get home?
Jules: Are you ok?
Truman: I have the flu, or a chest infection.
Jules: I am sorry to hear you're not well.
Truman: It's okay, I will bounce back.
Jules: Glad you're taking time to go to the doctor. Forget the web cam until you get better. I love your fighting spirit.

Can you believe it? I ask him again to get a web cam, he tells me he's sick and I let him off the hook. Also, why did he ask me how much I spent on the clothes? Was he trying to ascertain whether I had money or not by how much I would spend on myself? He claimed to have fortune and a thriving business and to have been in a long-standing relationship in the past. He had also offered to treat me to a spa, further indication that he was a man of some means. All of this seemed so wonderful for a lonely single mother like me. He made me feel somehow worthy of love and a relationship, which is something that, for me, was so elusive. It was not his money that drew me—it was the investment he seemed willing to make in me as a partner.

Falling in Deeper

We had another long Skype chat for an hour and a half. This was all happening in November and December, 2010. It was all very fast—I knew him for less than two months, but he either Skyped with me (without a camera) or spoke to me every day on the phone. Every time, I gushed to him in talk or text, feeling so confident in our connection.

Jules: Every time we talk I feel more and more connected to you. I like you so much. I am so excited and happy! It's a wonderful journey already and it's just the beginning!
Jules: I am so thrilled we found each other! It's our time!

I cannot believe I wrote this—I can't even remember doing it. He wasn't even answering me and I was rambling on like a fool to someone I had never met. How excruciating is it to read and share this? I still feel shame eight years later.

Some of that shame was already present. I didn't reach out to discuss the situation with any of my friends or family because deep down, I knew that they would tell me to get a grip and stop what I was doing. I did not want to hear this, so I kept it all to myself. At one point, I did briefly bring up the situation with my good friend Pam, and she made it clear that she did not think it was a good idea. Instead of taking her advice, I just kept quiet about it. In my mind, I felt she didn't understand, but in hindsight she was spot-on with her concerns and was just showing that she cared and was worried about me. My daughter would have had the same reaction as Pam if I had told her. I know deep in her heart she wants nothing more than for me to find a good man to share my life with, but if I had explained the situation to her in honest detail, she would have begged me not to go and meet him. My daughter is very tuned in to her intuition and this is something I admire in her. She seems to have the best instincts of anyone I know.

Meanwhile, lost in the fog of romance, I would sit up for hours, waiting and thinking of nothing but the positive.

Jules: I stayed up late last night hoping you would come online. Wish I didn't do that now. I feel very tired. Silly me!
Truman: Baby, please don't do that, go to sleep...
Truman: We have our whole life together.

I had sent him a getting-to-know-you questionnaire in the hope that he would send it back to me and I could learn more about him. Of course, he never sent it back, but I had filled it out for him and therefore had given him a load of information about myself that he could use to lure me into the fantasy world he had created: his construction job, his phone shop, being adopted and going to school in Canada, and even having a fourteen-year relationship with a woman. I assume now, given what I know, that all of this was untrue. My fantasy world was a love story with someone who supported me, loved me, and had shared interests. I thought our worlds were a perfect match, but I couldn't completely see this for myself yet, and the quiz was just a fun, revealing way to affirm this.

What I had given him was a tool kit for manipulating me further by connecting with me on things I cared about or was interested in. It's ironic that I meant to use this as a way to genuinely learn more about him and see if I could build a connection, but instead, by filling in the questionnaire for him, I was giving him ammunition to deceive me on a deeper level than he already was. The fact that Truman did not bother to return the quiz is just another red flag indicating that he was not genuinely interested in me, but I made excuses in my mind that he was just too busy with his two careers.

The quiz included deep-thinkers like 'What is your biggest fear?' and fun one-liners such as 'Who is your celebrity crush?' As I read my heartfelt and genuine answers that I sent to this stranger in the hope of making a connection eight years later, I feel a pang in my heart. It's not embarrassment I feel—it's sympathy. I just want to give that girl I was a hug and tell her that I am sorry she was so lonely and yearning for love. I'd tell her that I don't blame her for trying to find someone to love; it's a natural urge and desire.

Meeting Truman in Person

Not long before I was about to fly to the UK to meet Truman, we had this exchange on Skype. It includes another embarrassing confession: I love 'The Bachelor' (I am really baring my soul in this book!). I know some consider it 'trashy' reality TV and likely to be staged, but I find the whole premise of the show fascinating. I get hooked on the drama and romance, even though it is completely unrealistic. It's like being a fly on the wall; we get to see into other people's lives, and on some level, this is both riveting and entertaining, but it can also be a reminder of how good my life is. At other times, it can be a reminder of how alone I am.

Truman: Just been thinking all night.
Jules: What have you been thinking?
Truman: So much...
Truman: I was answering those questions you sent.
Jules: Oh cool, yeah.
Jules: Did you enjoy my answers?
Truman: It got me thinking how unhappy I am in my job...
Jules: I had fun doing it.
Truman: And not having love...
Jules: Well, there's hopefully a new beginning and new love just around the corner.
Jules: Fingers crossed.
Jules: It's quite exciting, hey?
Jules: I spent the whole day watching girls get their hearts broken on 'The Bachelor'. It's a very strange concept! It made

me think so much about how I want true love and someone to
share my life with.
Truman: It's more.
Jules: Everyone wants to have love in their lives, enjoy their jobs,
and have fun with their partners. Also doing things for others
gives you personal satisfaction.
Truman: I am making some changes in my life... for happiness.
Jules: It's all possible you know!
Jules: Glad to hear it! I hope I can be a part of it!
Truman: I know, babes.
Jules: Every time we communicate, I feel closer to you.
Truman: You are the foundation...
Truman: The primary reason...
Jules: Oh, that means so much to me.
Truman: You showed me something that I thought was only
in movies.
Jules: You are amazing. I feel so privileged to have found you.
Jules: I am looking forward to seeing your quiz answers. Thanks
for doing that. I am excited to learn more about you.
Truman: It was interesting.
Truman: Anything for you, baby.
Truman: I luv you...

Some of this is cringe-worthy, but it shows how dizzy
with excitement I was and how much I wanted it to work. I really
was living in a fantasy world, but I think that comes from years
and years of being alone and really wanting a partner in my life.
As humans we're not solitary creatures; we're designed to have
partners. I had been in two physically and emotionally abusive
relationships and been scammed before; I just wanted this to be
real. When you want something badly enough, you will believe
anything. It's amazing how I was able to convince myself that
this was real when the truth was that I being scammed on an
epic scale.

I didn't know at the time that the change he was talking
about was quitting his imaginary job as a project manager

because he now knew that I was coming to see him and he had lied through his teeth. When we were on the phone, he clarified to me that he had quit his project manager job. In our next conversation on Skype, he said, 'I am so happy I met you… and you made me give that job up.' I never once asked him to quit his job or even suggested it.

This was also the first time (but not the last) that he said that he loved me, and I felt uncomfortable with him saying it. I never expressed this concern to him, but it is reassuring that even in my desire for this relationship to work, there was still some semblance of logic operating in my brain, just not enough of it.

Truman: You know, you are a great person.
Truman: I am so happy I found you.
Jules: Oh, so are you.
Truman: I love you so much.
Jules: I think we are really lucky and have so much to look forward to.

I did not return this sentiment of love to him in any of my messages or when talking to him on the phone, although I spoke a lot about wanting to find love. I could not see how anyone could say they love someone without meeting them. It just doesn't make any sense to me. I was hopeful and having fun, but I did not have any feelings that I was in love with this guy. However, this is how scammers work; they want the person that they are communicating with to fall in love with them without meeting them. Thus, slowly but surely, I was giving away my heart, and with it my good sense.

One positive outcome is that I quit smoking. Truman hated smoking and I remembered how it played a role in my missing out on a relationship with Trevor from Shanghai, so I decided to quit before I met him.

One day, Truman noticed that I was not myself and asked if I was okay while we were talking on the phone. Coincidentally,

I wasn't okay, I was feeling low, and his 'perceptiveness' blew me away. This kind of deeper-level understanding of my moods reeled me in even further. I wrote this response to him:

Jules: I was just thinking, you are very tuned in to me already. I do feel a bit flat and tired today. I'm very impressed you picked it up. It's just another great sign of our connection!
Truman: I know…
Jules: I am really impressed! Not that I wasn't already impressed by you!

I can't believe I was so mushy and elated with someone that I had never met in person. What was I thinking? The fact was that, at forty-five, I was starting perimenopause, and this may have played a role in my mental state. I was grabbing a hot man instead of the hot water bottle I really needed. A woman's hormones often go haywire in perimenopause, and this may have made me more susceptible to this man connecting with me on an emotional level by appearing to show empathy towards me. My body and mind were buzzing and reorganising themselves in preparation for menopause, and I associated this intensity of feelings with the connection I had made with Truman.

We communicated throughout the two months that led up to my visit. We emailed (his were always very brief), talked on the phone, and chatted on Skype—still without a camera. There was more talk about him coming to live in Hong Kong, and then a Skype chat to remind me of his work in the phone shop. I want to scream when I think about the praise and admiration I offered him.

In this chat below, he mentions his last day at his imaginary construction site job. He also sets the scene for another layer to the scam—this portion related to Liverpool— that I was completely oblivious to at the time.

Jules: Hey Tru… what are you doing? Working in your shop or doing handover at your other job?

111

Truman: Just got back from Liverpool site...
Truman: Last day.
Truman: Really busy so will chat with you this evening.
Jules: Congrats on last day. How does it feel?
Truman: All my love for now...

Truman had offered to book a hotel for us for my Manchester visit, but when he got back to me, he suddenly needed me to do it. For some reason, in that moment, I lost all rational thought and I found myself booking the hotel.

Truman: Babes, can you sort the hotel out?
Jules: Sure, do we want it for all nights I am there?
Truman: It's affordable and next to shop.
Jules: Ok, I will do.
Truman: All nights... Yes, baby girl.
Truman: Thanks.
Jules: No worries.
Truman: I miss you.
Jules: Miss you too.
Jules: Wow... Friday 31st is really expensive... but oops, too late, already booked.
Truman: Should we get a cheaper hotel for that Friday night?
Truman: I am looking right now.
Jules: I think they will all be expensive.
Truman: Do you think it's too much?
Jules: We can cancel Friday night earlier in the week.
Jules: Should we stay at your place?
Truman: I will see if I can find an alternative.
Jules: Ok, it's up to you.
Truman: In case we cancel... is that okay?
Jules: I don't mind either way... no problem.
Truman: Just thinking of funds... I have put a lot into my shop...
Truman: Okay, you seem sleepy...
Jules: Whatever you decide will be great... I am easy.
Truman: We can talk in the morning.

Truman: Love you.
Jules: Sure...
Jules: Bye.

I like the way he cleverly made it seem like he would be paying for the hotel or at least splitting the cost. I felt a bit concerned, yet again, that he was saying he loved and missed me, but I brushed it aside and I responded that I missed him.

My Life in Photos

When I was a toddler with Mum.

Having a tea party with Nikki and her doll, Eve.

A little fight at the puddle. Nikki looks unhappy and I look smug.

Nikki, Sam and I in the garden on the farm. I am wearing an eye patch as I had a lazy eye.

The farmhouse where we grew up.

Inside the old Blacksmiths Shop on the farm.

The remains of the old Blacksmith's Shop after it was torn down.

Mum and Dad in the late 1960s.

At primary school with Nikki.

My siblings and I on the farm.

Sitting on the homemade go-cart surrounded by my siblings.

Reading at home on the farm.

At boarding school with two of my buddies.

With Dad in my late teens.

Acting in 'Pals' TV series in my early 20s.

In my cyborg costume for the film 'The Time Guardian'.

Working in Lux nightclub —aged 21.

My first modelling shoot —aged 19.

At my wedding with Mum and Dad.

With my brother Sam.

With Mari, both pregnant and so happy.

With my daughter.

On the little island in Hong Kong before I discovered internet dating.

My first profile picture for online dating.

With Pam at a murder mystery night.

At Universal Studios with the girls and Dean.

At a Chinese tea ceremony

The movie poster for "Mama's Home."

Hong Kong Confidential Podcast.

A recent photo of me at a friend's wedding in Boracay.

One-Sided Email Exchange

I talked to my daughter about Truman and the fact that I was going to meet him. I am sure deep down she had reservations, but she wanted me to be happy and still trusted my instincts. I never told her about the incident with Dean, so she didn't really understand my level of naïveté and poor judgement. She joked about meeting him to vet him as she was always amazing at intuitively knowing if someone was a good person or not. Even if my daughter had met him and warned me against him, I am not sure I would have listened to her. I certainly did not listen to Pam's warnings, which caused her annoyance and worry, I'm sure.

I sent Truman a few emails during the two months before my UK visit, and he rarely replied. When he did, his responses were very limited and brief: a song link, or just a couple of words. I thought it was because he was so busy with his two jobs, but his lack of response could support my theory that the person that I was Skyping with was not him. On Skype, he wrote a lot, and often. He still wouldn't Skype with me face to face, but he sent me pictures of himself. I suppose he knew I would have been more likely to realise that he was not genuine if we spoke face to face. It also could indicate that I may not have even been Skyping with him—it could have been anyone. This is even scarier to think about, and I will never know the truth.

Hey Tru,

Sorry I missed you online today.

I told my daughter about you last night. She was happy for me. She told me to tell you to come to her graduation next Tuesday so she can meet you first and vet you... Hahaha, she was only joking. She doesn't trust me.

Let me know as soon as you know if you get holidays... then we can plan our trip. How exciting.

Catch you later,
Jules

This is an email reply from Truman, the first one I had ever had from him:

I would love to go to the graduation...
Just a short reply...
I was really beat, went to bed early.

All my love,
Tru Buharay, the living legend

Can you believe he called himself a living legend? His ego was out of control and this was another red flag that I ignored like an ostrich with its head in the sand. I wrote:

Hooray!!!! I got an email from you... how exciting. Thanks! Even though it was short, it means a lot, you know!

That was funny regarding graduation, she was only kidding. Nice response, though! I will certainly visit you at some stage so you will meet her then, unless you want to pop to HK for Christmas?

I have printed up the picture of you in your shop, facing straight to camera, with your beautiful lips (and all). I love that photo, it's my favourite!

Thanks again for email, it was the highlight of my day. Can you tell I am easily pleased?

Anyway... have a great day and don't sweat the small stuff. (It's clearly a night for clichés.)

Warm hugs,
Jules

I didn't wait for a response before emailing again.

Hey Tru,

I wanted to just write you an email to tell you how much you mean to me and how lucky I feel to have found you. I am really excited to meet you in 11 days' time. I am so happy, I feel really calm and excited at the same time. Also, I was wondering what will happen, but it is great just knowing that this is the beginning of something really wonderful. I don't want this fabulous feeling to ever go away. I hope you still make my heart flutter when we're old and sitting on the porch in our rocking chairs playing with our grandchildren.

Truman, you make me smile so much!

Your girl,
Jules

Truman emailed me a couple of sappy love songs, and I noticed that the name he used in his email signature was different than the name that he used on Skype. He did not mention the name of the company in his email signature, which

I felt was also very suspicious. The detective in me was rising to the fore only to be shut down by the hormonal beast on a quest for love, denying all the clues that were hitting me over the head like a sledge hammer.

I took the emails as a sign of our growing connection, and I wasn't shy about how happy this made me. Encouraged by my response to the song he sent, he sent another corker. I wasn't actually into these sappy songs, but I told him I liked them because I liked the romantic gesture—even if it was more like being trapped in a Mills & Boon novel and I thought the songs were terrible.

In one of the songs he sent me were lyrics about a wedding, and he followed up by sharing his idea of an ideal wedding. This was a strategy to get me to think that he is open to getting married, which is what many single women my age want. This was not, and is still not, on my agenda. I am sure that this was another way for him to try to subconsciously influence me to think that we were made for each other. It actually had the opposite effect, and made me feel uncomfortable. It was too much too soon, but despite the over-the-top platitudes and gooey sentiments, it did not stop me forging ahead with my plans to meet him.

My daughter visited me with her boyfriend just a few days before I left to meet Truman in Manchester for the first time. I have always valued her opinion and she seemed supportive of my choice to go and meet him. Deep down, she has since told me, she was sceptical, but she did not communicate this to me at the time.

I believed I was on the cusp of a great new happiness, but on that trip, I reflected on my greatest joy in life: being a mother. I have worked very hard to give my daughter and myself a great life with many opportunities. My daughter has grown to become an incredible woman.

I wrote this to Truman a few days before I flew out to see him:

Hi Truman,

My daughter and her boyfriend are great. I was so excited to see them. We all had dinner in the village then came up here to my house. He is really great, just as I suspected.

Anyway, I am going to go to bed, we are all going for dim sum in the morning for breakfast. On Sunday we are all going to hike to the other side of the island and then have a Chinese lunch. Then we might get a speed boat back if we can't be bothered hiking back.

Anyway, I hope to see your beautiful face on here soon... hint hint!

Cheers,
Jules

You would think that I'd wonder why he didn't write much back to me, but I really didn't even give it a second thought. I just put it down to how hard he was working. We spoke on the phone or messaged every day, so the fact that he did not respond to my emails did not really bother me. I was too busy planning our future in my mind to recognise what was really going on right under my nose.

I didn't give up. I kept sending him emails despite his limited responses and lack of effort getting back to me. I also kept persisting with requests that he talk to me on Skype with a camera, but to no avail. I told him that I would feel less nervous coming to meet him if I could meet him face to face online before I came. He ignored this plea, and this should have raised great concern for me, but my plane tickets were bought and I was all set. I couldn't pull out at the last minute as I was invested and I really wanted to know if this could lead to something more. Here was a handsome guy who seemed to be very caring and empathic, was into me, and said he was willing to move to another country for love. In my fantasy world, this was what I was looking for, so I pushed all of my concerns and negative thoughts out of my mind and continued on my path to destruction.

I sent one final email before I flew to the UK. Notice the name I used when I sent this email to him, 'True Man'! Oh, the irony! It was like I'd had a personality transplant and was acting completely out of character.

Hey True Man,

I am on my way. Going to dinner with my daughter and her boyfriend then off to the airport. The flight is leaving on time. All systems go. I am a bit nervous, but really excited to see you. I assume you will be meeting me at the airport? If not, let me know and I will get a cab to the hotel; either way is fine. I will forward you my ticket again just in case. I will text you from Heathrow to let you know if the connecting flight is on time or if I have to hitchhike to you (kidding).

I will see if you're on Skype later when I get to the airport. See you tomorrow. (How freaky, that we will meet tomorrow!)

Cheers,
Jules

Well, there you have it. I was on my way to meet a man I met online. He had used two different names with me already, had an unidentifiable accent, and had never bought a camera so we could Skype face to face. He also told me that he loved me many times and seethed over his former love. He had two jobs that should have been full-time and it would have been very difficult to manage both, but he still found time for long chats—although he had rarely emailed me. I had only known him for two months and he had the worst taste in music ever. I was in for a shock when I arrived.

Manchester

I headed to Manchester, flying in from Hong Kong. When I arrived, there was a text from Truman saying he was really sick and asking if I could get a cab to the hotel, in the city centre, and he would meet me there. I waited in the hotel until midday (I had arrived at 7.30 a.m. on Monday 27th of December) and finally I called to see where he was. He said he had been asleep after throwing up all night.

Truman caught a cab down to the hotel and asked me to meet in the lobby. When I first laid eyes on him, he was leaning nonchalantly up against a countertop in the foyer and smiling warmly as I approached him. I was pleased to see that he matched his photos and was well dressed and very handsome. We hugged and he seemed enthusiastic, friendly, and very happy to see me. I was nervous but excited to finally meet him. He said he needed to run some errands, so we got back in the cab, which was waiting outside, and went to pick up a sign for his phone shop. It turned out that we could not pick up the sign because it was a public holiday, so we came back to the hotel.

When we arrived back in the hotel, he said he had forgotten his wallet and asked if I could pay for the cab. I was irritated and suspicious, but I paid. I later realised that getting me to go in the cab to get the sign was just a ploy to get me to go with him as he didn't have any money to pay for it. He would have known damn well that it was a public holiday and the store would have been closed.

Truman later commented on how I reacted when he asked for this money and linked my response to my past experience with scammers to explain my reaction. He would continue to link my previous dating disasters to my current reactions to things as the week went on. I really wish I had not told him about any of these past relationships and negative experiences, as he frequently used them against me during my visit.

He took me to his new phone shop, opposite a large shopping centre in the city centre, and also took me to his home. I met his partner, Jack, a short British guy with shaggy brown hair who was around fifty years old. This was the guy that Truman supposedly was arranging to rent half his shop. Truman only had one small counter in the shop, but he showed me all the stock he had in his house of the phones from his old shop that he recently shut down as he was moving to the new location. Upon reflection, this was all possibly stolen merchandise or empty boxes set up to look like merchandise with a few phones and accessories strewn around to make it look authentic. I also wondered later if the stock in his one cabinet in Jack's shop was even authentic. I didn't have a close look, and it may well have been fake or second-hand merchandise set out to add credibility to his story.

Truman told me he had hocked his diamond jewellery to a pawn shop in the Moston centre and the interest it was accumulating was a huge financial concern for him. He was also worried about the pawn shop selling it because the six-month deadline to buy it back was imminent.

Truman explained that if he could get his jewellery back he could sell it for a much greater value to pay off the rest of the lease on his new place and take over the entire shop. It wouldn't cover all of it, but it would be worth about eight or ten thousand all together, and he only needed £12,000 more to secure the shop completely. He would then be able to resell the shop quickly and be able to move to Hong Kong in the next three to six months. Truman assured me that he could then get on with selling phones and make loads of money. He did seem to do a lot of business when I was with him through calls and meeting people. He went inside the old phone shop on Moston's main street as he had the key, so I assumed it was his old shop as well, although it was empty. In hindsight, I wonder if he put a fake sign on an abandoned building. Did he really have a key? Was it already open? I don't know. It turned out the shop we visited is part of a very large phone company chain in the UK, so I think it is unlikely he would have owned one of the stores.

He told me I was beautiful and amazing; he was a complete charmer and really flattering. He was funny, intelligent, fun, and very handsome. He said everything that I wanted to hear. He wanted to live in Asia, travel to Africa, and initially gave me the impression that he had the financial means to do this. We slept together on the second and third days of my visit and it was very intense and I was falling for him.

When I first saw him without his shirt, I noticed a massive jagged scar right down the centre of his chest through his stomach. It looked like he had been violently stabbed or sliced like a large salami. When I asked him about it, he said that he had a liver transplant, and I believed him. Later on, back in Hong Kong, I researched liver transplant scars and they looked nothing like his scar.

On Tuesday the 28th of December, we went to hire a car at the airport, as he had been required to return his company car, a BMW, when he quit his job. I don't know why he didn't tell me it was an Audi, as that would have fit his story (the car in the photo he sent me was an Audi). Of course, this did not cross my mind at the time. He said he would pay for the hire car, but if I could put it on my credit card that would be really helpful because he only had a debit card. I agreed. He suggested that I rent it for seven days, as it was cheaper than for five days, and he could return it the following Tuesday, three days after I had returned to Hong Kong. We went in to make the transaction. I asked the car rental girl about insurance and had that added on to the contract. I also decided to just book the car until Saturday, when I was leaving, not Tuesday, as Truman requested. I didn't feel right about doing that when it was in my name.

I suggested that Truman add his name to the drivers list, but he refused, even though it was free and a simple process. I wondered why he wouldn't just hand over his licence and put his name down as a driver. I knew that if someone else drove the car and crashed it and they were not listed as a driver, I could have been liable for the entire cost of the repairs. He kept insisting that I follow what he told me to do, so despite my misgivings I went along with his request to be the sole driver on record. When we walked outside to the car, he became angry and yelled at me, saying that I was not working as a part of the team and that he knew what he was doing. He screamed that I should not have purchased insurance and that I should have booked the car until next Tuesday and he would return it. He was also mad that I had requested that he submit his name on the list of drivers. I could feel my throat growing tighter as I tried hard to hold back my tears. He was being so aggressive and wild that I felt fear in his presence for the first time.

In hindsight, I suspect that he did not want his name on the drivers list because he either did not have a licence or he did not want me to see his real name. I seriously wonder if he did not want me to get insurance so he could steal the car. I cannot think of another reason why he would not want me to get insurance when I was paying for it. I know how important full insurance coverage is, so it caught me off guard and made me second-guess all of the decisions that I was making regarding the car.

As we reached our respective car doors, the verbal onslaught was too much for me to handle and I burst into tears. Truman softened and walked around to my side of the car, hugged me, and explained that he had comprehensive insurance that would fix the car if it got damaged and that he didn't need his name on the hire contract. I was jet-lagged and confused. I knew he was wrong but couldn't be bothered arguing, so to my shame, I went back in and changed the contract and did what he wanted and cancelled the insurance. The girl at the counter could tell that I had been crying and gave me an empathic look.

I believe that she could see the hold that Truman had over me and the way he was manipulating me.

It was my first big sign that all was not right with the situation, but I let him charm me out of my fears. I had seen a very mean and nasty side of him, but he was able to allay my fears by going on a charm offensive once I had done what he requested regarding the car. On the way back to Manchester in the hire car, he was friendly and sweet and joked with me. He was trying his level best to get me on side and to forget about the incident at the car rental place. Sadly, I have to say it worked. My mood lifted and I soon forgot about how upset and concerned I had been.

His vomiting continued for the first day or two, and I bought him a lot of medicine. He borrowed money from me to buy a phone and only returned half of the money when the deal didn't go through. I don't know why I didn't challenge him on this, but I have always been pretty generous and must have been willing to let it slide. He took me to this great African restaurant in Moston where he lived, and I saw his cute little house, number 8 on a small street right off the main street next to a park and some estates. It was in disarray though, full of junk and phone equipment. It was in such a shambles that there was no way we could have stayed comfortably at his house.

Truman spun such a convincing story about how if he could just get the lease on his new shop and his jewellery back that we could have a great future together. He explained that he wasn't into public displays of affection, so he would not touch me when we were out, but he seemed very loving and comfortable when we were alone. He told me that he loved me and thought I was an amazing, kind, down-to-earth woman. He said he felt so lucky to have found me and felt that it was a new chapter in his life. These were all words I wanted to hear. This overshadowed any concerns that I had about the taxi payment issue, the hire car incident, and the scar on his chest, and I pushed all of these worries out of my mind. I basked in his praise and felt hopeful for the future.

I offered to lend him money to get his jewellery back. I could feel his excitement at this offer, but I misinterpreted this reaction as his connection with me growing stronger. He promised he would pay me back as soon as the shop was up and running and turning a profit. He assured me that he would be so busy given the amazing location of the new shop in the city centre and money would flow quickly into his business. I felt like I was helping our future. I had fallen for him over the two months on the internet to a point that when I met him, I was really excited, as he seemed so amazing.

One warning sign was a joke that seemed a bit odd in our first few days of meeting. Truman talked to my daughter briefly on the phone and showed an interest in her and joked about being her new stepfather. This warmed my heart rather than raising concern, because I loved to see our two worlds coming together. This response harks back to when my ex-husband used to say I lived in a 'Brady Bunch' world; well, this is evidence that he was correct. Like Carol Brady, I could see our little family coming together and the future seemed hopeful. I was certain that I would not be alone anymore.

With my trust reinstated in Truman, we went to get the money from the bank. The jewellery would cost about £1,800, then he needed money for rent on his old shop so he could have one month longer to sell the lease and then he would get £5,000. He also needed £300 for his sign for the new shop. I agreed to withdraw £3,500 pounds on the understanding that he would pay it back to me as soon as he had the money or he would return it in a lump sum when he sold the business to be with me in three to six months. In the back on my mind I could hear Dad, who was always incredibly sensible with money, admonishing me for this decision, but I silenced him and focussed on the future potential of this new relationship.

We had to go to four different banks around the city as the machines didn't work in two of them and one was just an ATM centre. I was starting to feel stressed and worried that this was not the right thing for me to be doing and was secretly relieved each time I could not get the money. The longer it took for us to access the money, the more time I had to think about the decision I made, and I started to second-guess myself. I was a single mum, with a daughter at university, and was solely responsible for both of us, and I was not wealthy by any means. I had the money he required, but once I had given that to him, I would not have that much left in the bank. Deep down, I was really hoping I could not get it. Truman insisted that we keep trying to find a bank where we could withdraw the money. He would not give up. The more I expressed my reticence, the more playful and loving he would become. He kept reassuring me that I would soon have the money back and that there was nothing to worry about. I was lulled into a false sense of security, and despite my misgivings, I went along with it. It was like I was drugged by the romance and his promises. I couldn't see the truth of what was going on. It's horrifying to reflect on now that I am out of the situation. What in the world was I thinking?

He was jubilant when finally I was able to withdraw the money, and as I handed it over to him, he exclaimed that I was his saviour and that God had sent me to him. Not only was his reaction so over-the-top that it added to my fears that I was doing the wrong thing, but I was also alarmed as he had said he wasn't a Christian but was spiritual. He had also been saying 'Amen' to indicate his agreement on different matters, but I thought that was just a turn of phrase. I had made it clear to him early on when we first started talking that I didn't want to date someone who was religious as I am an atheist and have had difficulties dating Christians in the past. Also, I had grown up in an atheist family, which is not uncommon in Australia, and I found some of the ideologies and beliefs associated with religion to be questionable and at times unreasonable. Although I respect everyone's choice to follow their own religion as long as it is not hurting others, I do not wish to date someone religious as I don't feel that our beliefs and values would align.

Hitting the Jackpot

Once Truman had the money we went straight to retrieve the jewellery from the pawn shop. It was gaudy and ostentatious and not my style at all. This just highlighted our differences and made me question my choice to be with this guy who appeared to be so overtly materialistic and driven by the accumulation of possessions. He was already wearing a diamond-studded watch that he said he would put up for sale after the New Year on Monday, once I had gone. He said that he wanted to enjoy it for a couple of days, and then he could use the money to pay me back. Pie in the sky, I realise now.

I thought it a bit odd to wear the watch and then to want to sell it, but I accepted that he liked it but needed the money. Why would a guy who worked for a multimillion-dollar construction company as a project manager and owned a phone shop have to pawn his jewellery? I was starting to seriously question things in my mind by this stage, but I had not made the connection between his supposed successful careers, his lack of money, and that these incongruities could indicate that he was lying to me on many levels. I just thought fleetingly, as someone who has never used a pawn shop, that this was a strange thing for someone of his supposed means to be doing.

The garish jewellery he recovered from the pawn shop consisted of a diamond ring, a cross necklace, and diamond bracelet. He also said there was one more necklace to obtain, but the receipt was at his house. In hindsight, this was all likely cheap, fake jewellery that he recovered from the pawn shop for much less money than he claimed, but this did not occur to me at the time. I also didn't flinch when he asked me to wait outside while he went in the shop to get it back. I should have realised he would not want me in there to see the true value of the jewellery or the name it was pawned under. This was a missed opportunity to gain clarity about what was really going on right in front of me. I was just so willing to believe his lies and follow his directions without question.

We ran into two of his friends and he bought a large bottle of alcohol. He had to go and see someone about a phone, so I went back to the hotel and watched television while waiting for him to join me. I waited for many hours for him to show up. At 9 p.m., he called to say that he and his friends were in the private lounge on the hotel floor we were on and they were having a party. He announced proudly that he had paid for dinner for his two mates before they all arrived at the hotel and this irritated me because I had not had any dinner and his lack of concern for me was evident. When I arrived, they were all chatting and drinking, and by the look of their drinks, they had been there for a while.

We had previously asked the hotel management about having a gathering in this private lounge on New Year's Eve and had been told it was for residents only. Truman ignored this rule and was happily entertaining his friends and enjoying being the host. I was a bit disappointed that he hadn't called me earlier to join them. They were clearly having fun without me. A combination of nervousness and rejection gnawed at my insides.

Truman was dancing around like a teenager, thrilled to have hit the jackpot with the cash I had given him. It occurred to me that he was so excited because of the money and now I was being cast aside somewhat, as he had what he wanted, and this made me feel very uneasy. His friends were nice enough, but my feeling deep down was that they seemed a bit dodgy, and this only added to my disquiet.

My intuition was quickly reinforced when Truman took off with his mate Treyvon and left another, Morris, with me. They did a 'job' helping out his mate for an hour, and then they returned with a brand new iPhone. Truman was flashing it around and giddy with excitement. I had a sinking feeling about the money and questioned why a guy who owned a phone shop would be so excited about a new phone, but I said nothing.

A waitress came over and asked for our room numbers. I gave mine to her and explained that the other two guys were with us. She politely said that just for future reference, the room was for guests only. I replied that I understood, was really sorry, and we were leaving soon. Then Truman went off on her, yelling that she was unprofessional for saying that in front of his friends and embarrassing me, and that she should have taken me aside, and that she was out of line. She went red and apologised, and I felt deeply embarrassed and sorry for her. I decided would call him on it later because he was very aggressive towards her, and it was completely unnecessary. The knot in my stomach grew larger.

We then all went out on the town in Manchester. Truman and Treyvon got rid of Morris because they said he didn't have any money and was a 'hanger on', which is irony at its best. Another guy, Moe, joined us and we headed to a bar with a young couple we met earlier in the hotel private lounge. When we got to the bar, Truman handed Treyvon £20 to pay for a taxi, and he left. Truman complained about him being a 'hanger on' as well.

While we were at the bar, I discovered that Truman was only thirty-six, not thirty-eight years old as he initially claimed. When I challenged him on this discrepancy, he said he lied because he wanted an older woman who did not want to have children. Now I realise he was looking for an older woman because we are often seen as the more vulnerable and easily targeted demographic who are likely to have money and no one to spend it on. I was forty-five at the time with a good career and an adult daughter, so I would have been his ideal catch.

The reason that I had discovered his age was that he was a bit drunk and super happy and flashed me an ID card with the name 'Sede' on it, not 'Truman'. I also saw his birth date. This was my first inkling that Truman may not be his real name. I had noticed that he had changed the spelling of his last name in the Skype chat when we first met, but I never questioned it; I suppose I did not want to alienate him, or perhaps I just assumed he was using a nickname on Skype. Now I was getting the hint that he used a different first name as well. When I asked him about it, he brushed the question off and changed the subject. He did not want to discuss this issue at all and quickly stuffed the card back in his pocket, realising his error in showing it to me.

We went to another club, and after a few drinks, Truman, who was very against smoking, as it was a deal-breaker for him, asked for a cigarette from a stranger and offered to share it with me. Crikey, this was not what I needed! I had not smoked all week and was trying to give up, but I succumbed to his pressure and smoked the cigarette with him. I thought his behaviour was very strange considering how much he had gone on about hating smoking. I just stored that red flag with the collection of others in the recesses of my mind. We moved on to another club and I bought all the drinks for everyone. While we were there, Truman gave me all the money to hold. He had sold the iPhone, so that money was in there as well. He also gave me £100 cash, which he owed me from earlier in the week, in some sort of magnanimous gesture to show that he was a man who paid his debts, but it was all my money anyway.

We left the club and caught a taxi. We got in and he asked the driver to take us to a fast food place, and the taxi driver questioned where it was. Truman went bonkers, yelling at him to take him where he asked and saying that he heard him, so get going. Truman's tone was hostile and condescending. I had already witnessed rudeness to someone working in the service industry with Dean, so these old patterns were rearing their ugly head again, and it made me feel uneasy to witness this rude behaviour. The cab then took us to the takeaway, and it was only a two-minute ride, so no wonder the driver questioned where he was taking us because we could have walked there easily.

Whilst in the queue, I decided to broach my concerns with him and suggested that he could still get what he wanted by using a different tone when talking to others. He snapped and became very angry, loudly arguing with me that his tone was fine and that the driver deserved it. We sat down to eat our food at the counter and he kept harping on at me in his fiery tone. Three women eating at the counter in front of us took it upon themselves to offer their opinions. One woman said we were both right; he felt he was being scammed by the driver and it was his right to be angry, but that I had a point as well. As she stood up to leave, she asked him where we were staying, and he named our hotel. She said to me, 'Oh, you're lucky, getting treated to that posh hotel.' I just shook my head because by now I knew that I was paying for the hotel. I didn't profess it out loud, but I motioned to her that I was paying. Truman saw this gesture and went off his trolley, storming out of the eatery and leaving his food behind. The woman looked shocked and said a quick sorry to me as I picked up the food and followed him out the door.

Truman was furious that I had embarrassed him in front of the women. He wanted to leave and demanded that I give the £100 back. I suggested we talk about it and convinced him to get a taxi with me. I was stalling for time to work out a way that I could hang onto my cash. He bellowed that he had decided to go home to his house, but I calmly convinced him to stay with me in the hotel, as I was only there for two more nights. I believed he was overreacting because he had been drinking, and I did not want my money to go anywhere without me. I was a bit drunk as well, so my judgment was poorer than usual.

Truman acquiesced and we returned to the hotel, the money still safely in my handbag. We went up to our room. Truman was still grumpy but had calmed down considerably. We got into bed and I tried to start a general conversation to move away from the drama of the evening and to lighten the tension. We started discussing the couple we had met in the lounge and who had come out with us. He said the girl was flirting with him, and that if he had wanted to, he could have had his way with her. He was very explicit in his description of what he could have done with her sexually and I could not believe what I was hearing. A decent man would never talk to his partner like that or disrespect another woman by sexualising her in such a degrading way. It was truly sickening to hear, but I am ashamed to say I was too exhausted to tackle him on this issue. I saw where confronting him had landed me last time, and I was not willing to stick my neck out again. I was tired and tipsy and just wanted to go to sleep and put this awful night behind me.

He asked for the money back and I reluctantly gave it to him, as I did not have any fight left in me. Then he told me he was going for a walk; instead, he went for a drive. He was drunk and driving the uninsured car rented in my name. I was starting to realise, once again, that things were not right and that maybe I should get out. My mind was racing, and I was feeling increasingly anxious and sick to my stomach. He came back an hour later and claimed that while he was driving around he was thinking about our future. He was softer, calmer, and more like his old self. He reassured me and then he fell into a deep drunken slumber.

As Truman snored lightly next to me in the bed, I ran through the litany of events that had caused me alarm over the past few days. The emotional and physical stress of the time I had spent with Truman had taken its toll on me. I was more nervous and anxious than I had ever been, I felt intimidated and scared, and it was difficult to think rationally. The drinking, the jet lag, and being gaslighted at every opportunity by this narcissistic man had messed with my mind and heart. I was conscious that I had a responsibility to myself and my daughter to rise above it and get out of this situation, and I needed to take action before it was too late.

Truman was truly a master manipulator: even now, I second-guessed myself and wondered if I was overreacting or being overly sensitive. All the kind and loving things that he had said to me swirled around in my head, and I searched for a glimmer of hope that my fears could be wrong and that maybe he was a great man after all, a man who could share my future. These contradictory thoughts and feelings are a real testament to the quality of the manipulation and coercion that Truman used on me. He was very good at this scamming business, and I was drowning in his artful exploitation.

Trapped in the hotel room, struggling with my confusion and fear, I made a hard and fast decision to get out. The bottom line was that I did not feel safe, and I was hopeful that I could still get away with most of my money, which I really could not afford to be losing to this conniving egomaniac. My heart was pounding out of my chest and I could feel it in my ears; I was afraid that he might actually hear it, too. I glanced at him sleeping next to me, and reassured that he was out cold, I carefully slid out of bed and started to quietly pack my bag. I tiptoed nervously into the bathroom and grabbed my toiletry bag, keeping one eye on Truman in case he stirred. I tucked it in the suitcase and slowly zipped it up, trying to not make a sound. Every movement had to be precise and slow. I did not want to knock anything over or make any noise to disturb his sleep. I formulated excuses in my mind at every point; if he happened to wake up, I would be ready for his inquiries as to what I was up to.

I crawled stealthily around to his side of the bed on my hands and knees. I was trying to breathe as quietly as I could. I felt the remainder of the money in the pocket of his jeans, which were on the floor. I carefully eased the money out of his jeans and slid it into my handbag. I carefully picked up the car keys from the bedside table next to Truman without making them jingle. My mind was a bit fuzzy from the alcohol, but I tried my best to keep a clear head. To me, my breathing sounded like a jet engine and my heart like a jackhammer on concrete. Would he hear me? Would I get caught? Can I do this? I was worried that Truman would sense my fears and wake up.

I was all packed. I had the money and the keys, and I sat on the bed shaking with terror as I tried to work up the courage to go. I was increasingly worried that if I didn't get out quietly without waking him that I would be in grave danger because I had seen how volatile he could get over the smallest things. The thought crossed my mind that I could be murdered in Manchester and no one would even know where I was. I had visions of him chasing me down the hall, catching me at the lift and pummelling me to death. Or if I went down the back stairs, I was afraid he might catch me and kill me with his bare hands and no-one would hear me scream. I was running different escape plan scenarios through my mind and I did not know if I could go through with it, but I had to try.

Just before I took my chance, it occurred to me that Truman might hear me open the door, so I went over to try it first to see how noisy it would be. I tiptoed over and slowly manoeuvred the door handle downwards as gently as I could, in the hope that it would not make a sound. Suddenly, there was loud click as the door opened, and he stirred. I froze, panic rising in my throat. In a drunken stupor, he asked what was going on. My mind raced and the answer came to me on the spot: I said I was just putting the 'Do Not Disturb' sign out and I grabbed it, hooked it on the outside door knob, and shut the door. He responded that it was a good idea and he rolled over went back to sleep.

My heart filled my throat and my head buzzed with panic and despair. My plan to escape with the money had been foiled. I sat on the end of the bed and felt like I wanted to cry. All my bravado and courage seeped into the floor as I considered my next move while he snored away. I was not sure I could get out quietly enough with my luggage. Should I leave it behind and run? I also was not sure where the car was parked, as he had just been driving it. I would have to pay my hotel bill before I left as well, and this would give him time to catch me if he awoke and realised I was gone. Where would I go, as it was the middle of the night in a city where I did not know a soul? I just didn't have the courage to go through with it with so many unknown factors that could hinder my escape.

I gave up on the plan and quietly put the money and keys back, opened my suitcase, and returned my toiletry bag. Defeated, I slid silently back into bed. I felt like I had failed, and that failure made me feel inadequate and pathetic. I could not slow my racing heart down; it took hours to regulate my breathing and heart rate. Even to this day, years later when I recount this part of the story to others, my heart pounds and fear rises in my belly, just like it did on that night. It's a visceral reaction that goes right to the core of my being. I feel dizzy and start sweating; my heart beats in my throat. It's one of the scariest moments in my life, and it runs like a horror movie in my mind.

The next morning, I confronted Truman calmly about his behaviour the previous night. He accused me of being abusive because I wouldn't give him the money back when he wanted to leave the restaurant and accused me of being manipulative. I suggested that his tone was too aggressive and that he should treat people with more respect. The discussion heated up, and I suspect that he sensed I was on the verge of leaving him and he changed tack. He sat down in a non-threatening pose and apologised to me. He made excuses for his behaviour and assured me things would be different once he could sort out his stress from his illness and his new business. He made promises about our future together, reassuring me that he would come to Hong Kong as soon as he possibly could and he felt that it would only be a few months and we would be together. Once again, he was charming, funny, and seemed to hear what I was saying and to acknowledge my feelings.

'You are all that I am looking for in a woman,' he said. I wanted so badly to believe in him. Perhaps I had misjudged him, and maybe he was being a jackass because he had been drinking. Could I have exaggerated everything in my mind? Which side of him was the real person? Could I be to blame for upsetting him? 'I'm not perfect, but you make me want to be a better person,' he said. 'Without you, I am nothing.' I am someone who normally puts others before me, but in this instance, not only did I consider his feelings before my own, but there was also something inside me that wanted to please Truman and to win him over. His tactics worked, and he had me right back where he wanted me in a matter of hours.

We packed up to leave the hotel to move to a cheaper place because that one was too expensive on New Year's Eve. We picked up his friend Treyvon and drove around looking for a hotel. I mentioned that I was feeling hungry and they agreed they could also eat. We arrived at a little hotel outside of the city centre and Truman suggested I go in, book a room and get some food, and he would see me shortly, as he just had to drop Treyvon off and come back. Once again, I was being sidelined for his mates or his business. This was becoming all too familiar.

I went in and booked a cheap but clean room and dropped off our bags. I went to the restaurant across the road and ate alone. The feeling of loneliness and being far away from home enveloped me. I felt like I wanted to cry, but I pushed these feelings aside and ate my lunch. Truman returned about an hour later and picked me up. I was surprised to see that Treyvon was still with him, but his next move was to drop Treyvon off at the train station and then he decided we should drive to Liverpool.

We had a great drive and got on brilliantly. He had a terrific sense of humour and said all the things I wanted to hear about how he felt about me. We had intelligent, stimulating conversation and laughed a lot. When we got to Liverpool, he showed me an apartment that he said he was buying and claimed he put a £14,000 deposit down on it but would need to secure a mortgage by the end of March to buy it for £128,000. It was a slick, black-windowed building right in the centre of the city near some amazing structures and it looked stunning. He did not take me inside to look at it or even stop to point out exactly which apartment it was. In fact, it looked more like an office building than an apartment building.

He stated that he didn't have a good credit rating and suggested that we should get a loan together to buy it. He talked animatedly about how much of an amazing deal the place was and how fabulous Liverpool was as a city. My heart was not in the idea, despite being impressed by the place. He said we would get lawyers to draw it all up and that it could be rented out and would be an investment in our future together in Hong Kong. Thank goodness I did not agree to do this. I was very noncommittal during our conversation and I could see he was getting frustrated by my lack of enthusiasm for his plan, but he was not going to give up. This was obviously the second phase of his scam and it was not working.

On the way back to Manchester, Truman kept going on and on about the way that we could build our future by purchasing this property together. I remember feeling a bit scared as he was driving too fast and quite recklessly and I felt unsafe and was beginning to notice how out of control this situation was becoming. I gripped the door and wished that I could press pause on the whole trip and take a moment to collect myself.

Luckily, we made it back to Manchester in one piece. Truman went to the shop to talk to his partner, Jack. I went into a bookshop next door and looked at some great books about old films while he chatted to Jack. I made a purchase and went to sit in the car and read.

Truman came out and called me in to talk with Jack about how to sort out the rest of the lease. He said that he had paid £3,000 for the lease, but £12,000 was still required for him to own the lease outright. He enthused that because I was his girl and now his partner that I should come and chat about the business side of things with Jack. I was a bit dubious, but I went in to the meeting anyway. This was another attempt to get more money out of me by showing me how legitimate all the negotiations were and how wonderful the shop would be when it was his. I remained very passive during the talk and refused to volunteer any assistance. Phase three of the scam, getting more money from me to pay for the shop lease, also did not work.

In hindsight, I suspect that Truman was never renting the shop and Jack was in on the scam for a cut of the proceeds. It's so odd that Truman just had one small counter in this clothing shop when he had not paid for the lease yet and had a house supposedly full of phone equipment. He was also apparently getting a sign made already for the shop, which we were going to pick up on the first day, but why would he get a sign made when he had not paid for the lease? To me, all of this just did not add up.

We left the shop with Jack to get some Chinese food to take back to the hotel. While Truman was in the takeaway shop, Jack causally asked me if I was helping Truman financially. I said yes but before I could say any more, Truman returned to the car and the conversation stopped. I don't know if this was his way of trying to warn me or encourage me to give more. He could also have wanted to know how much I was giving Truman to see if he was getting the correct amount as a cut. We dropped Jack off at his home and drove off, so I will never know.

As we were driving back to the hotel, Truman asked if there was any way I could just give him £500 more for his rent on his house because his cheque had not come through from the project management job that he had quit and he needed money for the phone shop sign as well. He said the cheque was late because he missed some days at work and that he would have it within a week. He promised that he would transfer the money from the cheque straight to me. I said that I wasn't sure, as I really did not want to do it. He reiterated how my financial support now would help our future together and reminded me how strongly he felt about me. He was highly skilled at bewitching and coercing me, because I finally agreed.

We sat and ate our food in the hotel foyer. Afterwards, he proposed that we go and get the money from the ATM. I said no and countered that we should do it the next day. He insisted that he would rather get it now, in case there were any problems. I was still hesitant, but he kissed me and playfully convinced me to go. I do not know why, as I really can be such a strong-willed and determined person, I did not stand up for myself in this situation. I absolutely did not want to give him any more money, but I was afraid of rejection and possibly even fearful of his temper given the aggression that I had witnessed during my visit.

We went to an ATM, but £400 was the daily limit on that machine. He was not satisfied, so he took me to another ATM and asked me to get the rest. I withdrew another £200. I have no idea why I gave him an extra £100. It was nearing the end of my trip, money had played such a big role in making him happy, and I must have still felt the need to buy his affection. Part of me believed that if I gave him more money, this would make him happier and have the knock-on effect of him treating me with more respect. In this relationship and others, I felt unworthy of real affection just based on who I was, and made up for this inadequacy by being overly generous. I have always been able to spend money on others much more easily than on myself.

Money in hand, Truman announced that he wanted to go to an all-night religious vigil for a couple of hours to commune with God and prepare for 2011 in a spiritual way. If that wasn't enough to confirm my fears about his religious status, he said that I should be happy that I lent my money to a man who believes in God, because he would have to pay it back or he would be judged. What an odd rationale! I still wanted to believe him; I hoped his conviction in his beliefs would compel him to pay me back, despite my deep-seated apprehensions.

Certainly, I was disappointed to spend New Year's Eve alone. However, because I was tired from the night before and didn't like his friends very much, I agreed to wait for him while he went out for a couple of hours. I went to bed and fell asleep. I woke at 1.30 a.m., and he was not there. I tried to text and call him but no response. I sent him a text saying I had made a mistake; I really needed that money and couldn't afford for him to have it. Unsurprisingly, there was no response to my text or calls.

I went back to sleep until 6.30 a.m. when I woke up and was horrified because he still wasn't there and he had the hire car, which was uninsured and registered in my name. My mind played back our previous experiences: meeting with Jack among the clothes racks over lease money, listening to a pitch in front of the black glass 'apartment' building in Liverpool, waiting outside of the pawn shop, reading 'Sede' on the ID card in the dimly lit bar, and on and on. My gut-wrenching fear of being liable for an uninsured rental vehicle made something click: I now definitively understood that I had been played for money, and this was all a scam.

The realisation burned brightly and painfully as now I could see it in the clear light of day. I felt sick—truly sick—with panic. Not only had I been scammed out of a significant amount of money, losing the car to theft or damage could cost me a fortune. I called my girlfriend Mari in Australia and told her what was going on. When I spoke to her, I was not crying—I was in panic mode and wanted her advice. I gave her a quick rundown of the whole week and the current situation. The fact that I was flying back to Hong Kong later that afternoon made everything feel particularly urgent, as I needed to get the car back as quickly as possible. My heart was beating like a drum and my voice was shaking but I was pretty calm and just wanted to see what Mari thought I should do before taking action.

Mari suggested that I call the Australian consulate or the Manchester police and ask for their help and advice. She reminded me to be really careful as I could be in danger and was all alone in Manchester. Mari gave me the strength to stay focussed and to do what I needed to do to try to get the car back and ensure that I made it out of this situation in one piece.

Cigarettes Saved My Life

I leapt up and went to the hotel lobby. I got the number for the Australian consulate and the local police from the guy at the front desk. I rang the Australian consulate in the UK and ended up speaking to someone in Canberra, Australia. She was great and told me to wait a couple more hours and then call the police and report the car stolen. She was very compassionate, straight-forward, and down-to-earth, in true Aussie style. I did not feel judged by her and she took me seriously. It was really nice to talk to someone in authority with an Australian accent; it was oddly reassuring as I was trying not to panic and was holding back tears.

My contact at the consulate wished me good luck, and I went to the service station next door to the hotel to get some cigarettes and a soda. I was so nervous that I suddenly needed a cigarette even though I had found not smoking during the entire week easy. I felt like it might calm me down a bit and give me a chance to relax and think straight about what I should do.

As I came back through the lobby, the guy at the hotel front desk asked if I was alright and why I was asking for the consulate and the police phone numbers. I told him I was concerned that this guy I had just met might be stealing the hire car, registered in my name and was asking for help and advice. He suggested that I also contact the car hire company and said he would get me the number. He was really kind and obviously concerned, and I was grateful for his help. I thanked him and went outside for my second cigarette in six days.

As I put my cigarette out in my empty Coke can, I noticed Truman walking through the car park about forty metres away. I jumped up and turned to walk inside and heard Truman call 'Jules!' behind me. I ignored it, slipped into the lobby, and told the guy at the desk that Truman had arrived and warned him not to say anything when he walked in because I was afraid the clerk would try to hand me the phone number in front of Truman.

I heard the sliding doors open and I turned around to greet Truman. He wouldn't speak and stormed past me towards the lift. I followed him up to the room. I knew that I may have just put myself in danger, but I was more afraid of losing the hire car. He still had the keys and I needed to get them. Standing silently with him in the lift, I became aware of his physical power. He was an imposing and scary figure, tall and heavy-set with fierce eyes and an aggressive and tense body language. I worried that I had let my concern over the car override my natural instinct to preserve my life. I had a terrible feeling that things were about to get nasty.

When we got into the room, he simply stood there, glaring at me. I causally asked him how the vigil was, trying not to let him hear the fear in my voice, and he kicked off. He screamed that I was a manipulator and a liar and that he had caught me smoking. He thought I had run back into the lobby because I was smoking and did not want him to see me. I claimed that I wasn't lying, as he hadn't asked me about smoking and I would have told him I had smoked if he had asked me. I denied running inside and said that I had not seen him and was just walking inside anyway.

I reminded him that he had smoked the previous night with me, and he said that was okay because we were together. What kind of warped logic was that? He accused me of smoking all week and lying to him, so I showed him the new cigarette packet with only one missing. He just kept bellowing at me, pointing his finger in my face, and calling me a liar and manipulator. As he edged closer and closer, I considered my options. I was aware that the hotel room was basically soundproof and I was possibly alone with this madman on an empty hotel floor. Sheer panic rose in my throat and my heart beat rapidly in my chest.

I inched backwards slowly and stood between him and the door. I really wanted to get those car keys back! He towered over me, spitting into my face as he screamed. I begged him not to hurt me. I shot a glance back at the door and held onto the inner calm and control that I'd long ago learned to embody in the face of a violent partner. Part of me was thinking, 'Oh crap, here we go again', and I thought if I just kept my cool, I could get through this scary incident as well. Given that I had experienced so much verbal and physical abuse in my past, I knew that I should not get angry or hysterical, as that would just escalate the situation and put me at much greater risk. I knew that I had to stay calm if I didn't want to be beaten to death in this three-star hotel on the outskirts of Manchester. I was relying on instinct to get the car keys back and get out alive. In hindsight, this was not a wise move; it was a huge risk to have gone up to the room with him, and no amount of money is worth risking my life.

I asked for the car keys back and he insisted that he would return the car on Tuesday, but I was determined to get it back. This was my main goal and I was not going to fail. I asked him again very calmly for the car keys in a rational and neutral voice, and for some unexplained reason, he violently threw me the keys. I caught them and held them tightly in my hand. I could not believe that I had them back. Then Truman lunged past me, knocking me sideways into the wall, and he pulled open the door with all his might. The swinging door smashed me face-first and crushed my whole body between the door and the wall like the stroke of a hammer. It happened so fast, I hardly registered the effect at all, but I screamed on impact and it took a few seconds for me to gather my senses.

I shakily followed him down the wallpapered corridor, as I knew that he had to get his belongings out of the car and would need me to open it. I also wanted to get out of the room and the empty corridor, downstairs to where people were and where I would feel marginally safer. I was still incredibly scared and realised that being alone with him up on the empty floor of the hotel was terribly risky. I needed witnesses and people around me who could call the police if things kicked off even more. My mind raced with possible courses of action to get him out of my life swiftly and safely.

When I arrived outside the lift, he was in it, with two small blokes pressing their backs up against the lift wall quaking with fear. Truman was still screaming abuse at me and calling me a manipulative bitch, amongst other things. While I watched from the foyer, the lift door closed, and I will never forget the image of two little guys looking at me with their mouths and eyes wide open and this big hulking man going ballistic at me as the metal doors closed in his contorted face. I quickly jumped in the other lift and he was waiting for me in the lobby. As soon as I appeared, he towered over me and started screaming at me again. He was swearing, calling me a liar and a manipulator and generally going crazy, gesticulating and throwing his arms around wildly. I remained totally docile and calm throughout all of his violent histrionics.

The guy behind the front desk, whose wife had now joined him, called out to Truman to stop swearing and threatening me. Truman then turned on them and started screaming. He advanced towards the front desk ferociously, yelling at the couple to mind their business, stating that he could do whatever he liked. He was pointing at them and roaring like a lunatic. They clutched each other and looked in fear for their lives.

I kept my head down and rode it out. He obviously didn't care about kicking off in public, and I was afraid of what that could mean. Thoughts of my daughter were flashing through my mind. I could not leave her alone in this world; I needed to survive not only for myself but for her. I could not put her through losing her mother at such a young age. I had to make it out of this alive, and my instinct for survival was strong. In a situation of high stress, we naturally either adopt a fight, flight, or freeze approach. I did not freeze and I did not flee; I stayed to fight, using my wits and courage to my advantage.

I went outside, hoping to draw Truman away from abusing the hotel staff, and it worked—he followed me out to the car. I stopped a short distance away from him and unlocked the car with the remote. Truman started to unpack the boot, all the while still yelling at me and swearing. I noticed a couple of new pairs of shoes in there and an awful pink jacket that I suspect may have been a gift for me, as we had planned to exchange Christmas gifts that day. He had clearly been on a spending spree and out partying all night, not at a religious vigil.

Truman had forgotten his bag in the room and he ordered me to go and get it. I went back upstairs and got his bag as fast as I could. I wanted to take back all of the medicine that I had bought him, but if he noticed, it could just tip him over the edge because he was right on the precipice. I left it all where it was and went back down to the car park with his bag.

My heart was pounding, but I maintained my composure. As I walked through the car park, Truman was watching me with a face like thunder, glaring at me intently with very threatening body language. I spotted a man out there having a smoke—maybe one of the guys from the lift. While walking at a steady pace so as not to arouse suspicion and let Truman know that I was speaking to him, I quickly and quietly said to the man, 'Please watch me, and if this guy starts to beat me, please call the cops.' He looked at me with a combination of fear and empathy and reassured me quietly that he would keep an eye on me. His kindness momentarily made me want to crumble and cry, but I snapped back to reality and kept moving.

I approached the car, handed Truman his bag, and asked him for the £600 I had given him the previous night. He replied, 'What money?' I answered, 'The money I gave you yesterday,' and he said it was all gone, that he had used it already. He aggressively offered for me to search him. In one last-ditch effort, I asked him about the other money that I had lent him, and he angrily yelled that he would pay it back as we arranged.

It was beginning to dawn on me that I may never see any of the money again.

Truman's anger and vitriol was rising rapidly and he seemed to be working himself into a wild frenzy. He said that I should 'F*** off' and that he didn't care if he went to jail. He repeated this three times in rapid succession. I thought that it was really frightening that he was talking about going to jail and that he did not care. It flashed across my mind that perhaps he had been to jail before, and this was a huge warning sign that he was really unhinged and just how much my life was still at risk. Even in broad daylight, with a guy watching us in the car park, I knew I still was not safe. This was my cue to back off as he seemed like he was about to snap completely.

I locked the car with the remote and then moved away quickly. I knew I was in huge danger but I had what I wanted, which was the car. I knew that I would never get the money. It was worth a try, but I had pushed him to the limit, and it was time to get away.

As I walked back through the car park, a taxi came to pick him up. He threw all of his goods from the boot of the car and his bag into the taxi and left. This would have been around 8.15 a.m. on 1st January. I had a brief cry out of relief and shock and thanked the guy in the car park for watching me. He said no worries and asked if I was ok. I told him that I was alright and that I appreciated him staying there and keeping an eye on me.

I then sat down in the car park near the hotel door and rang Mari, and we rejoiced over my lucky escape. I cried from relief and the terror of what I had just been through. We both knew that I had been very lucky not to be beaten or even murdered. Even though I had been in two seriously abusive relationships in my life, I had never felt like I could easily have been killed. I smoked about six cigarettes whilst talking to Mari and slowly calmed down.

Suddenly, it occurred to me that Truman might come back and that he still had a key to the room. My blood ran cold and my scalp prickled with fear. I knew I had to take action and this was not over until I was in the car and driving away from this hotel. I quickly said goodbye to Mari and went upstairs, grabbed all my stuff, and ran down to pay the bill. Adrenaline was still flowing through my body and I fully expected Truman to appear behind me at any minute. My mind was not helping me as it churned out the worst-case scenarios that could still occur.

I thanked the owners of the hotel profusely on the way out and noticed that the woman had been crying. She had clearly been frightened out of her wits by this monstrous, violent man, and I felt so sorry for putting her through it all. I thanked them so much again. They had really supported me as much as they could without putting themselves in grave danger. The best thing I could do in return was get out of there, so I left.

Lucky Escape

I jumped in the car and drove it to the airport. I was so relieved and joyful to have survived and that I had escaped with all my belongings and the car. I felt such enormous relief; at last, after a long and harrowing week, I could really allow the feeling of being finally safe to wash over me. I was almost euphoric to be free, and I felt completely secure for the first time.

I was so glad that the car wasn't damaged, except for a hub cap, which he may have scratched when driving drunk. The lovely girl at the car hire place remembered me from the hire day, and when I told her about the hub cap, she said not to worry. She was very sweet, as I am sure she remembered how aggressive Truman had been in front of her. I changed my flight to an earlier one to London and called my daughter. I briefly told her what had happened and that I was safe. She and her boyfriend sent a driver to pick me up from the airport in London, and they met me close to the airport at a lovely British pub.

We had a sombre talk covering the highlights of what had happened to me. At the time, I thought I had only seen a couple of worrying signs, for example, the way he spoke to the taxi driver, the hire car clerk, and the waitress in the hotel. The scale of the duplicity of this man had still not fully dawned on me, as I was in shock and had not had time to process everything. Now I can see that the whole thing from the dating profile to the New Year's Eve vigil was a set-up and a scam and that every single thing was probably a lie.

I even had the guts to tell them about the money I lost, which, apart from the risk I took with my life, is what I am most ashamed of. Truman was very good at what he did and had obviously done this type of thing before. I am sure I was not his first victim, and unless I did something about it, I would not be his last.

My daughter and her partner were so warm, loving, and supportive. They said my only problem was that I was too trusting and too generous. They both said that I was such a good person that I had been taken advantage of because I look for the good in everyone. They implored me not to worry about the money—the fact that I made it out unharmed was the most important thing. This was what I really needed to hear, and I was so grateful not to be judged or admonished by them. It reminded me of the way Dad supported me all those years ago when I crashed the car as a teen.

This incident certainly brought all three of us closer. I had only met her boyfriend two weeks earlier. I am so proud of her for her choice of men; she has always chosen well, unlike her mother. My daughter suggested that I go and see my therapist and that I would benefit from talking to him. I have worked with my therapist off and on to cope with being single and alone and the self-esteem issues that stem from that. I believe that talking to a professional can be a great idea and very useful to develop self-awareness and coping strategies.

My daughter also suggested that I should tell my friends what happened as they love me and would be supportive. I feel that she was worried about me going back to Hong Kong alone and not having support. I decided that I would tell them, but I would not mention the money, as I was so ashamed that I just couldn't do it. I would tell them the rest of the story.

I was particularly worried about telling my best friend Pam, as she clearly expressed her reservations and did not want me to fly all the way to the UK to meet this man. I had travelled to meet men before, but she had never expressed this level of concern. This was different—she was protective of me, and her gut instinct was that this whole trip was a bad idea. I was not looking forward to coming home to an 'I told you so.'

154

I believe that much of the shame I feel about this mistake stems from my upbringing. Dad was always very careful with money and encouraged his children to save and spend wisely. Losing money in a dating scam would cause my parents huge disappointment, as would, of course, the risk I had taken with my life.

I flew to Hong Kong that evening, feeling much better for having spent time with my daughter. Before take-off, I took a sleeping pill and slept for nine hours on the flight. I woke up in the cramped space and realised I injured my arm when Truman smashed me between the wall and the door. I fell back asleep and I woke again as we headed into Hong Kong, feeling very sorry for myself.

When I landed, I discovered that all of my buddies were eating lunch at Pam's house, and I called and invited myself up. It was around this time that I noticed the bruises on my hip, arm, and head. My jaw and my temple were hurting, and I discovered that my watch face was also smashed. Overall, I felt stiff and sore. It was like the shock was wearing off and the injuries that I had sustained were finally becoming more apparent.

When I got to Pam's, my friends all began quizzing me about my trip. I explained the significant events and talked openly about the violence; however, I didn't mention the money that I had lost. Later in the evening, I chatted in more detail to one friend and told her about the money. I also told my friend at work the next day. Otherwise, I left out the part about the money because I was worried about everyone judging me. I live on a small island, and didn't want to be gossiped about. Once the dust settled, I did tell most of my close friends about losing money, but no one knew the actual amount.

This story will probably shock most of the people who know me, even my closest confidants. After all, I have a successful career, a good education, wonderful parents and a daughter who loves me, and a life I am very happy with. Being conned in an internet dating scam was inconsistent with all of the other responsible and measured choices that I make in my life. I am a good role model, a community-minded citizen who cares about others and wants to make a positive difference in the world. The choices that I have made when it comes to men are somewhat out of character and something that I am not proud of. Matters of the heart can mean that responsible, rational thought processes can be pushed to the wayside in search of love and companionship. I realised the need to learn from my mistakes, and that this would be a process that would take some time.

The Aftermath

The next day, I went to work and put in a full day, giving vague details to a few of my closest friends who knew I went on the trip. Then I talked to some friends of mine in Australia about it online that night. They were great and told me to stop beating myself up and to be thankful to be home safe in one piece. One suggested that I do something healing or cathartic to help overcome the trauma, and I decided to write it all down.

As I was writing, it truly dawned on me that I had been swindled and deceived from the beginning, and I had been caught up in a major dating scam. Every single move he made was a part of his grand plan, right down to not insuring the car, not having a credit card, the bogus construction job, professing his love for me, the mates, the shops, and the jewellery. The fact that he would not email me or text much but only speak on the phone or on Skype—without a camera—were now clear signs of fraud and hinted at the possible involvement of many more people. It was all part of the dating scam plan of a seasoned predator who knew exactly what he was doing.

I called my friend from work who knew the whole story and cried my eyes out in dismay at my choices and the realisation that I was played like a fiddle from the start. Here it was, two days after I returned to Hong Kong, and I was crying and shaking, finally going into complete shock for the first time. I hadn't cried since I left the hotel with the recovered hire car, as I just switched into survival mode to get home and maintain damage control. It was great to have her there to reassure me while I had a meltdown. She talked me through my revelations and then I continued to write down my experience, moment by moment.

As a result of being scammed, I have promised everyone that I will never fly overseas to meet a strange man again. For a short while, I was still hopeful that Truman would honour his word and pay me back, but after putting the events down in black and white and doing that again from a legal perspective, I realised that I would never see the money—or him—again. I had to just let it go and pay the price, both literally and figuratively.

The hardest pill to swallow was that I made it so easy for him. He was clearly coming back with a new jacket for me, so I suspect that he intended to continue the charade and milk me for all I was worth. I am certain that he would have wanted to work on me partnering with him by financing the lease of his shop and also the mortgage for the place in Liverpool, neither of which I suspect really existed.

I thought he must be kicking himself that he messed things up so early because of me smoking a cigarette. Truman catching me smoking and consequently flying into a rage possibly saved me and got me out of a situation that I could have gone on longer and ended with me being badly hurt. That's if he was able to manipulate himself back into my favour after staying out all night—given my track record with him, this may have been possible. I may have gone back to see him at the end of January during Chinese New Year or bought him a flight to Hong Kong. We were also discussing going to Ghana at Easter. He probably would have turned up without money and I could have spent a fortune.

As it was, I was scammed out of £4,100 and paid for everything, including the hotel, car and food. I was violently assaulted, physically threatened and verbally abused.

Back Home

Taking Back My Power

Four days after arriving back in Hong Kong following the assault, I decided to make a report to the police. It was partly because now that I was back home and feeling in control again, I wanted to do something to stand up for myself. I did not want Truman to get away with what he had done to me or for him to scam any other women.

The statement told the whole story—in fact it was too much for the police requirements. I had submitted seven thousand words, and then cut it down to about seven hundred words, as they just wanted me to focus on the assault.

Halfway through writing my first version of the statement, I broke down in tears. By writing it all down, I was finally able to clearly see the warning signs I had missed and the web of lies he had woven. I felt so incredibly gullible and I cried and shook like a leaf. I called my friend Mari and she calmed me down with her words of wisdom and assurances that it was not my fault. On her advice, I took some calming essential oils and continued to write. It was very cathartic to get it all out and I was glad that I did it. I had started the healing process but I had no idea that it would take years to overcome the emotional toll that this whole ordeal took on me.

Initially, the UK police would not allow me to submit a statement from Hong Kong and said they could not help me. I did not give up and I rang the Manchester police and asked to speak to an inspector. Once I finally got to speak to someone at the top, they said they would accept my statement from Hong Kong and would move forward to arrest Truman.

After I made the report to the police, I was hopeful that Truman would be arrested in the next few weeks. In the meantime, I took photos of my bruises and went to the doctor to get reports on my injuries.

I often thought that I am very lucky that I am such a big woman; if I was very small, like many of my friends, then the injuries I sustained could have been much worse. I did have a constant tic or twitch in my right eye after the assault and this lasted for about three months. I went to a neurologist for X-rays just to make sure there was no major damage, and thankfully, there wasn't. Eventually the twitch and my other injuries went away, but the emotional scars were with me for a long time.

I believe that this whole ordeal must have happened for a reason, and perhaps that is not only to grow as a person but also to help other people not to make the same mistakes I did and help them recognise the warning signs or help them cope if they find themselves in a similar situation.

It has taken over eight years to record my story because I felt so much shame that I shelved it for years. I couldn't face the fact that I had been scammed and was so gullible and naïve. I was worried about the reaction of my friends and family when they read the book and realised full extent of the story. Until recently, none of my family knew about this story apart from my daughter and brother, Sam. He and I are very close, and he is someone I can talk to in great depth and is always completely supportive and never criticises me. I felt concerned about being judged, the repercussions of my choices, and the way people might view me in the community. I did not want to be seen as a fool, but rather someone who is courageous, reflective, and has learnt from her mistakes.

Recently, I went to a life coach, and that has helped me get to a place where I am ready to share. Also, beginning my podcast 'Hong Kong Confidential', where others share their stories, secrets, and personal journeys with me, has inspired me to have the courage to share my own. We all have to be heard to heal, and hearing the stories of others can somehow help us deal with the stuff that life throws at us. It's important to own our stories to be able to truly begin the healing process.

I had to go straight back to work and try to put the emotional trauma that I experienced to one side and focus on my job. I was able to do this quite well, as I love my job and it is my priority. I still had physical scars from the assault, but I was able to hide them under my clothes.

For the emotional scars, I made an appointment with my Chinese doctor for acupuncture to see if she could help me cope with the aftermath, in particular the feelings of shame and the nightmares I was having. I also met with my therapist, who was able to help me cope with the overwhelming embarrassment and regret I felt at the choices I made. I was very pleased that my friends were so supportive; I would not have been surprised if they had admonished me, but they didn't. I was very grateful for this, and I try to remember this generosity of spirit. If I am ever in a position where I might feel judgemental towards someone else for their actions, I stop myself and remember my mistakes.

In a bid to obtain closure, I wrote an email to Truman. I knew that I would never see the money again, but I thought it was worth a shot to ask him anyway.

Dear Truman,

Here are my bank details so you can transfer the money. You owe me £4,100. Payment of £600 should be made this week when you get paid.

Please send me a quick text or email to confirm when the payments have been made.

Thanks,
Jules

This was his response:

You are a liar. You lied that you don't smoke for me to come and catch you smoking and you run off into the lobby of the hotel. You made me quit my job making a good income on your pretexts. I then invested in a phone shop thinking I would be starting a life with a truthful woman... to find out that it was all a big lie. To make things worse, you went back on your promise for me to use the car until Tuesday, taking a hire car from me in the middle of the night. I had to start putting all my items on the street. All because your true colours came out after I found out. All the time I was smelling smoke on your breath, you had been lying to my face. I lost my Vertu phone that night due to your falsehoods and have lost a lot more due to your lies. The money given has gone into the business as agreed and I may be going back to look for a job because now I realised I was a big fool to quit my job to spend time with a phony, pretentious liar. You said the money was in good faith in a fake relationship and due to your lies the money is lost and my money is all down the drain. You owe me £12,000 for my Vertu phone. I know you have taken it. You owe me for making me quit my job knowing very well you were still smoking. Knowing very well that I would never invest in a future with a smoker and liar.

How dare you contact me with bank details, when you have left my life in total turmoil here and have my phone. Kindly make arrangements to give my phone to my mate in Hong Kong who will post it to me. He will contact you once he confirms with me that you have agreed to give my phone back... but most importantly there is no remorse for your cold, mean, and selfish actions.

Truman Buhari

My heart raced as I read this email. It was not the response I had expected from him. Many panicked thoughts were flashing through my mind. He has a friend in Hong Kong? Surely that is not true? What if it is true? Could he find me? Am I in danger? He has my business card; could this affect my job? What is this crazy con man really capable of? Surely this is blackmail and against the law? His email made me panic and imagine a multitude of worst-case scenarios. I was worried that he was even more crazy and nastier than I first suspected, and I didn't know the lengths he would go to try and get more money out of me. I did not expect this, and initially I was scared out of my wits.

I was in the middle of reading Katie Piper's book Beautiful. Piper is a strong, inspiring woman who suffered at the hands of a maniac. Her perpetrator raped her, held her captive and threatened her life. When he decided he didn't want to be with her anymore, he stalked her and threw acid on her face, disfiguring her for life. Her story is inspirational, but also a stark reminder of how lucky I was. It appeared from this email that Truman wouldn't just let me go, and I wondered if any of these outcomes were still a possibility for me.

I forced myself to get a grip and think rationally about the situation. He was on the other side of the world and did not have the financial means to come to Hong Kong or to find me. Thankfully, he did not know my home address. I doubted that he had a friend in Hong Kong, and even if he did, could they be convinced to harm me when he could not even pay for their services? I know that it is easy for a bully to make threats hiding behind a computer, and I was hopeful that they were the empty threats of a seasoned con man's final attempt to extort more money from me.

I sent the email he wrote to the police as he admitted to taking my money in it and I felt that this could support my case. A Vertu phone is very expensive—it retailed for about US$30,000 at that time—and I'm sure this claim was just a way to extort more money from me. I certainly did not have it or even know what it was; I had to search for it on the internet to find out as I had never heard of it.

I told the police that Truman's accusation of phone theft was a lie and I included his home address in the email. I was really proud of myself as I was able to find his exact address using my memory of where we went and an online map. I also gave them the location of his old phone company and the shop where he had his little counter with Jack.

PC Rick Hall from the Public Service Team responded by asking for another statement. I had sent them a rather long statement previously, but this time, they wanted it to be more precise and to provide the time of day, what was being said, and how I came to be hit with the door in as much detail as possible. I created a new statement and wrote back, apologising for the length of my previous statement but justifying it as part of my case to demonstrate that I had been swindled. I asked whether being swindled or defrauded was considered a crime and how the police would proceed from there.

In response, the police asked for photos of my injuries and to have those injuries documented by a doctor for medical evidence and thanked me for my cooperation. He was not particularly helpful in answering my questions, but that didn't stop me from asking more.

Dear PC Hall,

Here are the photos of the visible injuries on my left forearm and right hip. I also have injuries to my right temple, right side of my jaw, and left hip, but there are no visible signs of these. I have been having headaches this week. I will go to the doctor later today and get the report and email it to you as soon as I can.

Please let me know how you plan to proceed with the case. Can he also be questioned, held accountable, or charged for the internet dating scam, as I assume this must be a crime as well? Aren't there laws against fraud or swindling and false representation? He has admitted to taking my money in the email I sent you. Please clarify.

Thank you for your kind assistance.

Regards,
Jules

While the police were processing my documentation, I did my own research and learned that I was caught up in what is known as a Sweetheart Scam, where victims are often duped out of their life savings and can end up with emotional scars. People often feel so ashamed that they do not report being scammed to the police and may not even seek help from family and friends.

Anyone can be a victim of a Sweetheart Scam; ethnicity, gender, age, social status, and level of education have no bearing on whether someone is likely to be scammed. According to Scamwatch, an organisation in Australia that provides information to consumers and small businesses about how to recognise, avoid, and report scams, 161,528 people reported being duped in online dating scams in 2017. Losses totalled $90,928,622 and the number of men affected was only slightly less than the number of women.

The con artists who perpetrate these Sweetheart Scams are professionals and it is often the primary way that they make a living. Like Truman, they have the ability to make people believe them, trust them, fall in love with them, and give them money. They listen to you, size you up, and then say whatever they can to capture your heart. Then they will promise anything in order to receive money from you.

Truman did all of these things, and he did them really well. Like many scammers, he groomed me by saying that he loved me way too soon and turned what we had into a whirlwind romance. He told me things that I wanted to hear and was very tuned in to what was important to me. Although I handed much of this to him on a platter with my long, informative emails and the getting-to-know-you quiz, he was still very adept at the scamming game.

Once you are emotionally invested, scammers will often ask you for a loan for a business or to help with an illness or an emergency. They may ask you to go in on a business deal with them or buy a property. Truman did all of this, including setting the scene for an illness or emergency as he did when he told me he was sick and throwing up. He did not actually use this aspect of the scam to full effect because he was busy running all of the other scams.

Often, when a Sweetheart Scammer feels that they have squeezed all that they can out of you or that you are not playing along nicely with their manipulative game, they will just vanish or pick a fight with you. Truman picked a fight with me. I surmise that on the one hand he was getting frustrated that I did not go along with the Liverpool scheme and I did not offer to go into partnership with him with the lease on the shop, but on the other hand, I still don't think he was ready to give up trying to swindle me. That's why I feel lucky that he caught me smoking; it made him so angry that it tipped him over the edge and he went crazy before he had really planned to end it. I saw the light, thankfully, and made my escape.

What I read in my research provided some relief. The blackmail at the end of the whole ordeal was a typical phase of the Sweetheart Scam, a last-ditch effort to see if he could get any more money out of me before he gave up. Truman's interactions with me were very much the formula of a traditional Sweetheart Scam. I would find out later just how much of a professional criminal he really was.

The Police Finally Take Action

For years I have been seeing an amazing Chinese doctor in Hong Kong. I received acupuncture and Chinese medicine from her not only for my injuries but more importantly for treatment for the trauma and nightmares I was experiencing. This aided me a great deal, although the nightmare of being about to flee the hotel room with the money would recur occasionally for years to come. She also counselled me at each of our sessions and played a significant role in my swift recovery from the whole event. She was kind, non-judgemental, and skilfully helped me to accept that I should not blame myself. This was incredibly helpful in the recovery process. She assisted me on an emotional level more than a physical level, as the physical scars were healing relatively quickly.

Like my Chinese doctor, my therapist addressed the root of my shame and helped me to overcome it. He is a Jungian psychotherapist and has a very gentle and calm approach. He has an intuitive, compassionate, and healing nature and delves deeply into the aspects of ourselves that hold us back. He was very adept at guiding me to try and understand why I made the choices I did and some of the reasons why I was unable to see the truth of what I was getting myself into. These sessions helped me begin to forgive myself for my mistakes.

As soon as I had them, I sent the police my medical report and copies of the photos of my physical injuries. I also sent evidence from the bank withdrawal that I made in the UK to prove that I had given him the money.

I did recognise that without any form of written contract, there would be virtually no chance of getting my money back. I just wanted the police to know I had been swindled out of this money by an internet dating scammer. I felt it was important that they knew this and had the bigger picture. If Truman was to continue to perpetrate the same crimes against others, there would be evidence of his previous behaviour. A lot of my motivation for following up with the police was to let Truman know that he had messed with the wrong woman, to inconvenience him at the very least, and most importantly, to protect other women from falling victim to his internet dating scams. I clearly was not his first victim and I assumed that I would not be his last.

I sent this email to Truman to try and placate him by saying I was searching for the Vertu phone that I knew never existed and make one more attempt to get my money back:

Hi Truman,

The email you sent me accused me of stealing a phone. You did not say anything about it being left in the car. I will call the car hire company tomorrow and see if I can get it back for you.

Please can you pay me back the money I lent you? The bank details are below. Please can you honour your agreement?

Thanks,
Jules

Truman responded with this email:

I need that phone back ASAP. You did not honour your agreement to let me use the car until Tuesday, making me lose my customers phone… but you don't care about that or that I have to buy a £12,000 replacement phone. I want that phone back or you will pay me the difference. You did take the phone when you took the car back forcefully. Now give it back before I start making phone calls all over Hong Kong letting them know you are a selfish thief and a liar. If you don't get me the back the phone by this weekend you owe me £8,000 approximately. You are upsetting me with your selfish emails and calls concerned about your interests only. Where is my phone?

So now Truman was attempting to blackmail me, adding another manipulative string to his bow. I was worried that he would contact my work and make up a bunch of lies about me to discredit me in my workplace.

I went to see my one of my senior leaders at work to explain to him what had happened and give him a heads-up in case this deranged con man did have the audacity to call my school. I presumed that he wouldn't follow through with his threat, but I wasn't sure, so I decided to pre-empt his attack and speak to someone at work first.

As you can imagine, having to confess to my colleague the thoughtless mistakes that I made and the danger I had put myself in was particularly embarrassing. I cried as I told him what happened, and he sat transfixed by my story, clearly unable to fathom how I could have been caught up in such a serious scam. It was only a couple of weeks after the fact, and I was still very much recovering from the shock and trauma of it all. I had seriously let myself down by making these choices and allowing myself to be fooled.

Luckily, he was so kind, understanding, and supportive that I need not have worried. He reassured me that he empathised and understood, and I felt a huge relief that he did not judge me or scold me for making such idiotic choices and putting my life at risk. Of course, he hoped that I would learn from this mistake and never get caught up in such a scary situation again. The bottom line was that he had my back and would be ready if Truman called the school to slander me in his blackmail attempt.

I let the police know about the threat of slander and blackmail attempt. I was hopeful this would strengthen my case and inspire the police to take action swiftly. The nightmare was still continuing, and I had not expected blackmail as the grand finale.

Dear PC Hall,

Please see an email below that I received today from Truman Buharay (Buhari) threatening to slander me in Hong Kong if I did not pay him money for a phone that he supposedly left in the hire car the day I left Manchester on 1/1/2011. A car hired in my name and paid for by me. I checked the car when I returned it and there was no phone and I never saw a Vertu phone in his possession at any time, nor did I take it. This phone cost $30,000 in the USA; how would he even be in possession of such a phone when he needs to borrow money from me for his rent? His claims are preposterous.

He is trying to extort more money out of me and is threatening to slander my name in Hong Kong. He has my work details and may follow through with his threats. I did not take a phone from him and will not be giving him any more money. This is all part of his plan to ensure that he does not have to pay the £4,100 back that he owes me and is now trying to extort more money from me.

I called him on the phone yesterday 24/1/2011 to ask him to repay the money he owes me. He claimed to have left the phone in the car. (I have a poor recording of this conversation.) My emails requesting that he pay back the money that he owes me are below his. I sent this after the phone call. I said I would contact the car hire place to humour him as I know that he is lying and there never was a Vertu phone.

So now he is guilty of assault, fraud, and extortion. Surely he needs to be dealt with by the police. This will most certainly happen to other women.

Clearly, this man is a megalomaniac and needs to be stopped.

Kind regards,
Jules

I was frustrated that I was not really getting anywhere with the police. I got hold of an inspector by phoning and asking to speak to someone in charge, and then things actually started to happen.

I re-sent all of the evidence, my initial statement, my medical reports, and also key emails from the other officers. I was very thorough and ensured that the inspector would have everything that he needed to make a case against Truman. It was almost like this was part of my healing process. To be able to take back some of my power and to try to use my skills and abilities to convince the police to take action was very rewarding and empowering for me.

Finally, the police accepted my revised statement. They let me write it in Hong Kong and send it to them on an official form. They typed it up, signed it, and sent it back to me to confirm that it was correct and sign every page. I felt relieved that they were finally taking the case seriously and was glad that Truman could now actually be arrested and charged. This was a small but important victory for me, and it would not have happened if I had not been persistent and gone to the top with my requests.

Quite a bit of time had been wasted in trying to convince the police to allow me to make a statement from Hong Kong. I am a very efficient person who likes to have everything done quickly (just ask my friends—they joke about how quickly I do things all the time) so I wanted action taken as fast as possible. I even found the name of the African restaurant nearby that he went to every week and where he had taken me for dinner. If the police couldn't find him at the home address I provided, perhaps they could find him there. I also gave them all the names that I was aware that Truman used and sent them pictures of him once again, just to be sure.

However, despite having all the information they needed, any action they were planning to take seemed to be a long time coming. Five months after the incident, I sent a rather frustrated email to the inspector and one of the police officers who had been working on my case.

The police replied with this email:

Jules,

Arrest attempts will continue until he is in custody. He is known to the police on our systems from 2009 and the photograph taken from this time by the police is most certainly him. On the police system, he is a named suspect for the crime against you.

Regards,
PC Hall

I was delighted with this news, but at the same time it made me shudder to think that I had been mixed up with a seriously dangerous criminal.

My next email from DC North just reinforced this scary fact. He assured me that everything was in place for the arrest and interview of Truman, and numerous arrest attempts had been made at the addresses I provided. He added that 'should Truman come to the attention of the police anywhere he will be arrested.'

After this exciting news, I didn't hear much else, so I sent another email and did not receive a response. They must have been getting a bit annoyed with me, but I was like a dog with a bone and I did not want to let it go. I wrote to all of the police involved in the case once again in the hope of an update. These emails were sent early June, nearly six months after the assault, fraud and extortion attempt. The inspector in charge of the case replied that the investigations were continuing, and he assured me they were on the job. I was feeling disappointed that things were not moving quickly when I had provided the police with so much information.

Action Stations

Finally, after about six months, I received an email telling me that the police had forced the door in at Truman's house. Although he was not there, I was pleased to hear this news, as they were taking action at last. I also smiled at the thought of Truman arriving home, shocked to find that his house had been raided. Even if he did not know that it was because of his criminal activity with me, I was glad that his life was being disrupted. I am only human, and given how much he had disrupted my life on both an emotional and financial level, there was a part of me that was pleased that he was being inconvenienced as well. I just wished he knew that the raid was related to his treatment of me.

Jules,

For your information, PC Langston attended the address of Truman last night and on this occasion forced entry into the address as he believed Truman was inside. The house was searched and nobody was located.

There was documentation to suggest that Truman is still currently living at the address therefore roll over arrest attempts will continue. He has circulated on the PNC (Police National Computer) Nationwide as 'Wanted'. I'm sure the front door hanging off will no doubt make him aware we are on his tail now. Also, just to let you know without disclosing too much information, Truman as you know him is known to the Greater Manchester Police as Buhari-Obi Jabari Bosede.

On the police national computer he has got in excess of 20 alias names NOT including Truman, which appears to be his latest name (no doubt until arrested again).

He does have the distinctive scars, etc. to confirm it's him and he seems to travel around the country, judging by his convictions that stem from the late '90s.

Regards,
DC North

I was so thrilled that after all this time not only had the police raided his home, but they had also given me his real name, part of which he had used in the alias with me, and I could also see where 'Sede' had come from on his business card.

I was shocked that Truman had more than twenty aliases and a rap sheet dating back to the 1990s. I knew I had been dealing with a con man, but I did not realise the vast extent of his criminal history.

A couple of weeks later, I received another update from the police saying that Truman had been arrested whilst driving in a car on Sunday 22nd of August, 2011 by the Oldham police. The Manchester police provided all the evidence I had sent to them to this police force. They also told me that London Metropolitan police had been in touch with them and they were also looking for Truman in relation to another matter.

The Oldham police interviewed Truman and he told them that we had been involved in an argument, but that he just moved me aside to leave the room and had not assaulted me. The police said that the evidence I provided was consistent with Common Assault and was sufficient, but that unfortunately, they could not charge Truman because he was arrested after the six-month time limit allowed to proceed with the case. I felt some small satisfaction knowing that Truman now knew that I had pressed charges against him and that I had not gone off back to Hong Kong and done nothing, but I was gutted at the news that he was walking free.

I wrote back to DC North, expressing my appreciation but also my disappointment that he could not be charged.

Dear DC North,

Thanks for the email and your update on Truman Buhari's arrest. It seems very unfortunate that he cannot be prosecuted due to his arrest being longer than six months after the assault. This is particularly upsetting due to the fact that I feel that I was given the run around in the first few months after reporting the case on the 4/1/2011 and that the issue did not appear to be taken seriously until I made a complaint to Inspector Daniels in March and he insisted that an investigation take place. I feel that I was marginalised initially because I was not in the country and was told that I could not prosecute Truman from Hong Kong.

I do appreciate all of your efforts, support, and communication in the last few months, but it seems unfair that Truman cannot be prosecuted due to the time limit expiring. It's disappointing that this crime is being dismissed due to the fact that the police could not locate Truman despite me giving his home address, two work addresses, and an address where he regularly eats dinner, on the 4th of January when my complaint was made.

How he was not arrested earlier is beyond me. It seems to me that this issue was not really taken seriously until you identified who he was and realised that he had over 20 aliases and had a criminal record dating back to the late '90s all over the UK.

This must be a huge boost for him and I worry about him doing the same thing to other women. I was in fear of my life and I do not want this to happen to anyone else. I am sure if I had been severely maimed or hospitalised from this attack, the police would have taken things more seriously. The bottom line is, I was assaulted and injured, I was defrauded out of a significant sum of money, and he tried to extort more money out of me by threatening to tarnish my reputation in Hong Kong. This is unacceptable, and the fact that he has been arrested but not charged due to a time limit is outrageous, particularly given his criminal history.

Thank you for your time and efforts.

Kind regards,
Jules

I also sent a complaint email to the PSD, the Professional Standards Department of the Police, and received a swift response saying they would have the investigating officer present all of the evidence to them. The one thing that really stood out to me in their email was this paragraph:

The injuries on you were recorded as a section 47 assault not a section 39 (Common Assault). The injuries detailed on the crime do not have a six-month requirement to be presented before the Magistrates court.

It appeared that there was not a six-month limitation on an assault case, so now I was feeling quite confused and frustrated. Had I been fobbed off by the police? Had they misunderstood the statutes of limitations of the law regarding assault? I really did not know what was going on.

One thing was for sure: Truman knew I was behind the police's efforts to arrest him. I was disappointed at the confusion about limitations, but also grateful that I was so far away from him if he was going to continue to walk free.

The Outcome

Despite the PSD saying there was not a six-month limitation on prosecution, I was not convinced that I could go through with a court case when I lived in Hong Kong and would have to go to the UK to attend court. I could not get the time off work or afford the time or money it would take to see the case through to the end, so I decided to let it go. It seemed impossible to chase him successfully from the other side of the world, and anyway, I felt that I had made my point.

After a number of years away from this book, I felt resilient enough and that enough time had passed to allow me to return to it and share my story. It's not easy to put something out into the world that shows your personal weaknesses and foibles. I am a strong, intelligent, well-educated woman, but there is something in my personality that allows me to be treated badly by men. Why am I missing the ability to trust my intuition and the courage to care for myself and keep safe? It has to come down to self-esteem and self-worth.

Reading back over all that happened—from the Skype conversations to my police statement and emails—has allowed me to be a little less judgemental of myself and my actions, which I did not expect to happen. I can see the personal growth unfolding before my eyes, and it gives me a sense of self-respect. When I started writing this account in the tumultuous days after my escape, I was emotionally scarred and terribly upset with myself, so it was very hard to write. Today, I can share it with a sense of pride.

This is Me Now

Menopause

Menopause is the midlife point of a woman's life, where the first half is dedicated to merely survival (of oneself, and of the next generation) and the latter half is her 'actual/true' life (where wisdom blossoms). One can only really come into that true life by virtue of examining the lessons accumulated during the survival years.
This is at the same time a shift of the Yang into the Yin.
– Cecelia, my Doctor of Traditional Chinese Medicine

From the safe and secure world of my childhood to the perils of internet dating, after the final event with Truman, I found myself creating a brave new ending where I was taking responsibility for my actions and putting myself first. I was no longer prioritising finding a man as I wanted to enhance my life in other ways. I learned some hard lessons and I was going to put them into practice in my daily life. There were many changes that I was making in my life at a time when I was going through the biggest change of all.

I started perimenopause, the transition period that begins several years before menopause, around the age of forty-four, and I have been in menopause since I was forty-nine. I decided to go down the natural route of treatment for the effects of perimenopause as I had been seeing an acupuncturist and Traditional Chinese Medicine practitioner for years and always felt that this treatment method worked well for me.

Menopause is often a time of tremendous hormonal, physical and emotional changes. It released me from the constant desire for a partner and enabled me to focus on developing other aspects of my life and the relationships I have with friends and family.

Some women have very few symptoms during menopause, and others suffer greatly through the hormonal changes that can bring about hot flushes, mood swings, night sweats, itchiness, anxiety and depression, just to name a few. I sat somewhere in the middle of this spectrum and found some aspects of menopause very difficult and others a bit easier.

Being perimenopausal at the time I began talking to Truman was not ideal and I believe that I was influenced, to some degree, by my hormonal fluctuations. Looking back, my behaviour is a bit baffling as I am usually such a logical person. It is clear from personal experience and my research that not only was I more vulnerable to overtures of love, I was also wearing rose-coloured glasses and unable to see the red flags. I feel that oxytocin, known as the love hormone, also played a role in affecting my ability to make sensible decisions. Thus, experiencing a combination of perimenopause and oxytocin release meant that I was more susceptible to rushing into a connection with a stranger. I feel that the interplay of these forces, along with a desire to find true love, affected my behaviour and ambitions, and played some part in allowing myself to be duped. Women's endocrine systems certainly can influence their thoughts, behaviour and feelings, and I feel this happened to me. It is not the sole reason I was swindled but I believe that it played a role in my demise.

Now that I am on the other side of menopause, I feel more centred, like I am coming into my wisdom. I have more self-confidence and life experience, and worry less about what others think of me. This may be due in part to my hormones levelling out and not causing so much chaos, thus providing a sense of stability and calm. I have channelled my nurturing mothering skills into other aspects of my life. Many menopausal women begin new careers or hobbies and their priorities often change. I certainly have changed my focus and interests; in particular, my creative pursuits have expanded while my physical sporting life has slowed down.

I wish that it was more socially acceptable to speak about menopause so that women could get the support they need from friends or colleagues. Menopausal symptoms can be at odds with self-confidence and the image that women may want to convey to the world. A greater understanding and more open dialogue about menopause could be very helpful to women as they go through this significant change in their lives.

Motherhood has been the greatest joy of my life, and I love my daughter with all my heart. Being a mother has taught me to be more selfless, to think about my priorities and the true meaning of unconditional love. My daughter helped me through menopause by being understanding, thoughtful and supportive. She is vegan, and a yoga teacher and always encourages me to live a healthy and meaningful life. She has wisdom and knowledge beyond her years, is a wonderful guide for me and someone I can always turn to for advice. I don't know where I would be without her.

China Adventure

*What a humbling, uplifting, and empowering experience
we had in Guizhou! It was an adventure with soul and felt
so good to be contributing on a grassroots level. Jules's
energy, enthusiasm, and sheer, unadulterated terror on the
bus will never be forgotten!*
– Pete

In my mission to give back and focus on others, I wanted to do something challenging and inspirational during my holidays rather than embark once again on my perpetual search for love online. The social isolation of internet dating played a role in me stepping away from my friends, and I realised it was time to change my priorities. My reality for some months had been my connection with Truman, and thankfully I felt the need to move away from the desire to find romantic love and work on forging links with both my friends and the community.

The opportunity to do just this presented itself the first summer after being scammed by Truman. My girlfriend Pete and I decided to go to China to do a week of community service and teach one hundred educators how to teach English. We travelled up to Yanhe in Guizhou Province by train and then by car. It was my first time being driven in China, and I was shocked at how dangerous the driving seemed. In fact, I found this aspect of the trip the most stressful. Teaching one hundred adults how to teach English was a breeze by comparison.

We were working for a Hong Kong charity and eight of us were running the teaching program. It was a huge success and it was great to be able to use our everyday profession of teaching to inspire teachers in China. The adult students were so appreciative and willing to learn that it was very rewarding. However, given that some of them could not speak a word of English and Pete and I could not speak Mandarin, it was not easy at times. Luckily, some of our team members could speak Mandarin, so they helped translate for us.

Pete and I were standing outside our hotel one afternoon having just finished a day of teaching when a crowd gathered around us. One woman in the crowd could speak English, so she was asking us questions and translating our answers to the crowd. They were genuinely interested in our stories and were lovely. We had the crowd laughing at our silly antics and the fact that there was a huge language barrier did not mean that we could not connect with people on some level. This was a wonderful lesson in forging cross-cultural connections through humour and body language.

On this trip, I ate some Chinese delicacies that I had never encountered before. I tried a thousand-year-old egg, gizzards and an interesting fungus. I felt that while immersed in the culture, I should at least try everything that I was offered. This is indicative of my adventurous spirit that is sometimes a good thing, and sometimes, clearly, is not.

On our way back from Guizhou Province in the van, it seemed that the driver did not care what side of the road he was travelling on. He was overtaking on blind corners and generally putting all of our lives at risk with his careless driving. Whenever he pulled over for a stop, he would just stay parked on the road right after a corner or a hill while trucks and busses would come careening up behind us and have to swerve around our vehicle that would appear out of nowhere in their paths. I could not believe that anyone would take such ridiculous risks. Mind you, when you think about the risks I had taking in the past with men, this attitude seems somewhat hypocritical. On top of that, many others were also driving in the same reckless manner. It was so stressful to be a passenger in this situation. I did not cope very well at all.

I asked our guide and translator to tell the driver to change his driving, but it did not make a difference. Finally, I burst into tears and made the driver stop the van. Again, he just stopped in the middle of the road. We all got out and I was crying, saying that I did not want to die on the roads in China. Once again, I asked the translator to tell the driver that I wanted him to stay in the correct lane, stop speeding, and not overtake on blind corners. I made it clear that I was very stressed, upset and afraid for my life. Fortunately, this dramatic crying scene seemed to get through to the driver, and he drove more responsibly. Thankfully, I had learned from past mistakes to speak up when I was uncomfortable or afraid. I was making progress. Everyone else in the van thanked me for my outburst, as they were all very scared as well but did not have courage—or perhaps it was not culturally acceptable for them—to complain or share their fears.

Pete and I bonded during this week teaching English in China and connected with the organisers, the students and the locals. It was so nice to travel with someone who treated me as with respect, had my back and was great company to boot. Who needs a man when you have wonderful gal pals? I was asked to go back and do the same work again for the next few years during the summer, but as much as I loved the experience, I could not go again due to the danger I felt when driving on the roads. I could not put my life at risk like that again.

'Mama's Home'

*Our 'Mama' made the set feel like home, and with a
bunch of professional strangers around, there was
nothing better than that.*
– Nikhail Asnani, Writer/Director, 'Mama's Home'

'Creativity is food for the soul', and I decided that I
needed to have more of it in my life. Creativity nourishes me
and makes me feel better about myself. Being creative fills a
void, and I am discovering talents I never knew that I had. One
of the creative pursuits that I have always loved is acting.

I received an email from a former drama student,
Nikhail Asnani, saying he was a filmmaker and was making a
short film, 'Mama's Home', in Hong Kong, and he wanted me
to star in it. I was flattered and of course I said that I would
love to be in his film. I ended up helping with some aspects of
production and so was also credited as a producer, which was
an honour.

I played the role of Geena, an ex-con just released from
prison, who turned up on the doorstep of her son's house to find
that he was married... to a man. Geena was fine with her son
being gay, but her son's husband was not so thrilled to have his
ex-con mother-in-law in the house.

It was so exciting working on this short film and it took
me back to my youth when I worked in film and theatre. I was
working with two of my lovely former students and a wonderful
cast and crew. I did struggle to remember my lines on the last
day of shooting, as I was getting tired from the long days. Other

than this minor hiccup, it all went smoothly and the film was a great success.

'Mama's Home' is an eleven-minute short film that went on the LGBTQ+ short film circuit and ended up winning awards in many places, including film festivals in Nevada and Amsterdam. It has been screened in many cities around the world and was well received.

Our very talented director Nikhail had this to say:

A force that brings the set to life, our 'Mama' was not only a producing partner but a cheerleader that made my first directing experience unforgettable. She pushed away doubts and her support pre- and post-production for the community and art is something Hong Kong definitely needs more of. Even though I was the director, she taught me a few lessons which have made me a better filmmaker today. No wonder she was everyone's favourite in high school—well, it's that or the fact her doppelganger is Lucy Lawless!

The film was being shown at the Kansas City LGBTQ Film Festival when I was visiting my daughter one summer in Canada. We decided to fly down and attend the premiere. What a hoot! It was such an incredible experience to not only represent our little indie film at this festival, but also being part of the screening was a real honour. We were treated like celebrities. The organisers gave us gifts, took photos with us, and walked us down the red carpet. At the end of the screening, I was invited onstage to talk to the audience and answer some questions. They were so enthusiastic and asked loads of great questions about the film and Hong Kong. Overall, this was a unique, once-in-a-lifetime experience, and to be able to share it with my daughter made it even more special. This was such a great way to spend my holiday; the traumas of past holidays were just a distant memory.

Rog-Raiser

My life was literally upside down, I did not know which way to turn. If it wasn't for Jules taking control of the situation, I don't think that I would have made it back to the UK in one piece.
– Donna

After focussing on trying to find love for so long without success, it was time to focus on my friends and family and to appreciate the positive impact they have on my life. Sometimes, when we're searching for something we believe is missing from our lives, we overlook the wonderful people and opportunities right there under our noses.

When my dear friend Roger, who lived on our island in Hong Kong, was diagnosed with stage four melanoma, it was a huge shock to his family and our little community. He was married to one of my closest friends, Donna, and had three children aged from seven to twelve years old. Roger was given only three months to live by the doctors in Hong Kong, and everyone was devastated. Donna and Roger's families were in the UK, and they learned about some new treatment options there that might help Roger. As much as Donna and Roger loved living in Hong Kong, they needed to move back home.

Not only was the family dealing with this devastating news, but the financial pressure was mounting as they realised that they did not have the means to pack up their lives and move the whole family to the UK. Donna was understandably overwrought as Roger was her rock and her love. They were a strong family unit. Donna relied on Roger to help with the kids, who were a rambunctious lot at times. She was afraid for what the future would hold on many different levels.

Roger dealt with his diagnosis with humour, grace, and dignity. He was unbelievably pragmatic and stoic about it. I am sure he and Donna shared private moments of fear and uncertainty, but publicly, Roger was incredible. I guess he also wanted to be that way for his kids to make it as easy as he could on them and Donna. I have never seen anything like it.

I wanted to do something to help, so Donna and I brainstormed ideas that could help the family afford the move back to the UK, where Roger could get great treatment and they would have support from their extended families. We came up with the idea of Rog-Raiser, a fundraising event with the aim of making enough money to achieve our goal.

We spoke to a generous friend who owned a restaurant in Central, Hong Kong and he provided us the venue, staff, and food for free. I could not believe how supportive and kind he was. Then we had bands volunteer to play at the event. Also, Roger's generous colleague and some of his friends offered us several holiday destinations to be put up for auction.

I created a poster and we invited everyone we knew in Hong Kong to come to the event. It was a huge success. Roger was not there as he was already in the UK getting treatment, but Donna attended and the turnout was amazing. We raised over HKD$200,000 and this allowed the whole family to ship their belongings, buy flights, and rent a place when they got to the UK. One of the most wonderful aspects of living in Hong Kong is the generosity of the community here and the willingness of people to help others in need, whether it is a family like Donna and Roger's, a charity, or a community service event.

I also helped Donna pack up her whole house and supported her with the kids and in her preparations to return to the UK. We sold loads, packed up everything, and arranged the shipping as well. Donna was amazing during this time, as she had so much on her plate, yet her beautiful positive spirit shone though.

Jules made everything bearable, and I can't thank her enough for all the support she showed my family. She organised the Rog-Raiser in Hong Kong, which made moving back to the UK stress-free regarding the financial side of things. This is not something that we wanted to have to worry about when we were moving our whole life and family to another country. We are so lucky to have such good friends in Hong Kong. I love you, Jules!
– Donna

Roger lived for another four years in the UK and he may not have had the same amount of time with his family if they had not returned home. In fact, at one point, he went into remission due to the great treatment he was getting.

When Roger passed away, we held a memorial on our local beach at the same time the funeral was happening in the UK. We built a bonfire, and many of Roger's mates came down to say goodbye. It was a lovely event where we shared stories about Roger and had many laughs and tears whilst celebrating his life. We let go of some floating sky lanterns and I sang a song as the lanterns were released. It was a beautiful, poignant evening that I will never forget. Roger will always be in my heart. Rest in peace, Roger!

My Accident

I hadn't quite believed her arm was broken, because surely people didn't just stand up and walk around when they'd just sustained that kind of horrific injury. 'How the hell did you manage to do all that with bones sticking out of your arm?' I asked her, awed, and she shrugged. 'It had to be done, so I did it.' This pretty much sums Jules up.

– Rahat

Having been through a number of tough experiences in life, I have built a level of resilience that I did not really appreciate until one Sunday, on a hot summer's day, when it was put to the test. I was lying at home on the couch watching television and decided to meet my friend Rahat at the beach. I jumped on my bike and started to head out. There aren't any cars on the island where I live, just small paths for bikes, pedestrians, and the very tiny emergency vehicles. I live up a huge hill, so it is a downhill ride to get to the beach.

As I was turning down the path near my flat, my back tire slid sideways and I fell, head-first, towards the cement base of a light pole. I put my left arm out and landed with my hand on the cement block, which prevented my head from hitting the ground. I sat up after the fall and my left wrist did not feel right at all.

There were a few people around and one of them, a friend of mine, tried to help me. As I was sitting on the ground, I grabbed my left hand with my right one and moved it to see if anything was broken. Pain shot through my whole body as both my radius and ulna popped upwards away from my hand.

They did not break through the skin, but I could see they were badly broken. I asked my friend to lock up my bike and looked at my phone to see there were only ten minutes left until the next ferry. I decided to get on the ferry and get to hospital. I did not know whether the clinic on the island would give me a painkiller injection and there was an hour wait between this ferry and the next. I did not consider that a broken wrist would warrant me being transported in a helicopter to hospital, so I decided I needed to catch the next ferry.

I jumped up and grabbed my bag, held my broken wrist across my chest, and started to walk swiftly down the hill. I rang Rahat, who was waiting at the beach, and started to cry. I told her I could not make it because I had broken my wrist.

With her usual impeccable manners, Jules called to apologise for not being able to meet me on the beach. Anyone else would have stayed put and done a lot of shouting and fainting while waiting for an ambulance. Jules, on the other hand, had a clinical discussion with me about the angle her arm was sticking out at, while calmly walking herself to the ferry a kilometre away, getting herself onto the boat, sitting through the half-an-hour ride, flagging down a taxi, deciding which hospital would be best, and walking in the front door. For an hour, she gritted her teeth and did what needed to be done, on her own, in intense pain. When I saw the X-rays later, I almost felt faint myself, I couldn't believe how mangled it was.
– Rahat

I was in so much pain but was determined to stay focussed on my goal of making it to the ferry. As I got closer to the ferry, tourists were streaming down the pier, so I had to hang up on Rahat to ensure that no one bumped into me. That would be an added level of pain that I could not stand. I walked ahead, waving my good arm in front of me to get people out of the way. I was also crying a lot, so people could see that something was wrong and they politely moved out of the way.

I sat on the bottom deck of the ferry and sobbed heavy tears as the pain was becoming unbearable. I remember seeing many astonished faces staring at me, wondering what was going on. A young girl asked if I needed help. Through my tears, I asked her to request a bandage from the ferry staff. She returned with a triangle bandage and I asked her to also find a roll bandage, and she came back with one. I am well trained in first aid, but I was not thinking as well as I should have been, so I did not consider finding a newspaper or something to use to splint my wrist. However, I bandaged up my wrist and put on the sling to support it, all the while crying like a wounded beast. As I was finishing, an older Chinese lady got up from her seat and kindly reassured me by patting me on the back. Suddenly, the ferry lurched and the old lady grabbed my broken arm to steady herself. The pain shot through me like a knife. Through my tears, I asked her to stop; I appreciated her kindness, but I just wanted her to let go of me.

I called an ambulance, but they said that they could not take me to a private hospital, only the closest public hospital. This would have been fine, as the hospitals in Hong Kong are excellent, but there may have been a long waiting time in the public system, and I needed a painkiller as soon as humanly possible. Through my tears, I called a friend I work with and asked her which hospital I should go to. I just could not think straight.

When the ferry docked, I gently eased myself into a cab. I was trying to say the name of the hospital to the taxi driver, but he could not understand me through my tears. Thankfully, a man who lives on my island came to the rescue and popped his head in the window to tell the taxi driver the name of the hospital. At last, we were off. It's amazing how small gestures of kindness mean so much when you are in crisis.

On the drive to hospital, I called Rahat back and she tried her best to keep me distracted as I cried and cried. I was not hysterical, but big, heavy, full tears were pouring out of my eyes. Rahat told me she called the hospital to tell them I was coming and asked them to give me a painkiller as quickly as possible. I was so grateful to have Rahat on the phone during the whole journey as I did not feel so alone. She kept me laughing through my tears and asked me to tell her about a dream I had mentioned the night before to keep my mind off the excruciating pain.

I arrived and was whisked straight in to the doctor, and without even examining me, they gave me a shot of pethidine. Suddenly, the pain eased and I could breathe again. The tears dried up and I felt peaceful and pain free. I called my daughter to tell her what had happened and she offered to fly back to Hong Kong to look after me. I told her not to worry and to stay at university. I also messaged my colleague to tell her I would not be at work the next day and asked her to arrange cover for my lessons.

I was taken to see a specialist, who just happened to be one of the best hand doctors in Hong Kong and was on duty in the emergency department that day. What good luck! It had taken me one hour to get from the accident site to the hospital. It was one hour of the worst pain I had ever experienced and I still can't believe that I did it all on my own, with help from two friends on the phone and the girl on the ferry. This experience made childbirth seem like a walk in the park. I suppose the difference is that when you're having a baby you know the pain will be over soon enough and that something wonderful will appear at the end.

The doctor said I needed an operation and I was admitted. By 6.30 p.m., I was on the operating table to have three pins and a plate put in my wrist. The doctor said my wrist looked like I had been in a car accident and fixing it was a long and complicated procedure. My wrist never fully recovered, and I have osteoarthritis to remind me never to ride a bike again. Serendipitously, my bike was stolen just a few weeks after the accident. The universe was telling me my cycling days were over, and I should accept that there are a few things that I cannot do anymore. Broken wrists and broken hearts have much more significance when you are older and are to be avoided at all costs.

Life Coaching

Deep bow of respect to you, Jules, for seeking out and showing up to do the inner work we did together for you to reconnect with the creative, confident, vibrant parts of yourself that had been tucked away and forgotten about.
– Natalie Goni, Life Coach

Never one to shy away from seeking support, self-reflection or activities that can enhance my life, I was thrilled with a Mother's Day gift from my daughter in early 2017. It was a mindfulness workshop, where I would experience a day of well-being, positive energy and support. I loved this very healing and rewarding experience. I particularly liked Natalie, the woman running the course, and later in the year I decided to see her for some life coaching.

Initially, I went to see her because I was quite stressed about the way I felt I was being treated by some people in my life. A number of people would sometimes have a go at me or not treat me very well because I am not great at dealing with conflict, so I can be somewhat passive when challenged and feel I make an easy target. If a conflict arose, often I was shocked and unable to come up with a swift response to protect myself or challenge the way that I was being spoken to. I felt like I could not find my voice when I did not agree with someone or did not like the way they were speaking to me. I decided to go to life coaching to build my self-esteem, look at my patterns of behaviour and try to make some positive changes.

Natalie was incredibly helpful regarding this issue, and I have taken specific actions based on the work I did with her.

These changes in my approach have all been well received by friends and colleagues. More importantly, I feel better about myself. I found that when I say how I am feeling in a calm, measured manner and am not aggressive or disrespectful, most people listen and take on board what I have to say and adapt accordingly. This has been such a useful tool for me and has served to enhance my relationships with others.

The focus of our life coaching sessions then turned to my loneliness and life without love, my fear of missing out (which stems back to high school), and the fact that most of my friends are couples and at times this can highlight how alone I feel. I decided to do something to fill my time rather than watching television, which was how I often spent time when alone. I wanted to do something creative and expand my horizons. I was also thinking about my future, as I knew that I would not want to stop working at sixty when I will have to leave my current organisation, so I was considering my professional options. Subsequently, I thought about the fact that I had developed a huge love of podcasts and listened to them daily. During menopause, I used podcasts as way to help me sleep as well as for education and entertainment, so I loved podcasts for many reasons. As I worked through all of this with Natalie, I realised that I wanted to begin my own podcast—and that's how 'Hong Kong Confidential' was born.

Life coaching helped me become focussed on my goals, feel better about myself, find my voice in difficult situations, accept life as single woman, and develop my creative side. Overall, it was a really positive experience and something that I will do regularly. Life coaching also helped me get to a place where I was ready to take a risk, face my demons, and finish writing this book.

You showed the curiosity, courage, love, and tenacity to do what you needed to give us your true, wondrous, radiant self! I can't wait to read the book in full.
– Natalie

'Hong Kong Confidential'

The show about a woman from the country in South Australia talking to interesting people in Hong Kong steadily built an audience and hit new milestones. This is due in no small part to Jules's work ethic and likeable personality.
– Liam Carter, Auscast Network

After completing four sessions of life coaching, I started my podcast by signing up for an online course on an app on my phone. It was very affordable and run by a young guy from Melbourne. I completed the twenty-one-hour course in two days and made notes on the whole thing for future reference. I learned how to edit a podcast by watching video tutorials online. I downloaded the editing program, bought the recording equipment, and began to search for guests for my show.

I decided to do an interview-style show, as that is the type of podcast I most enjoy. I had listened to so many podcasts over the past few years and knew very clearly which podcasting conventions I liked the most, so I used these as a starting point for creating my podcast. I wanted to do interviews with interesting people in Hong Kong.

The best part about doing my podcast has been all the amazing and inspirational people I have met along the way. I have been astounded by the impact many of the people I interviewed have had on me. I have learned so much about myself by listening to the stories of others. This is one of the main factors that inspired me to complete my book: I realised that if others could share their innermost secrets or wisdom with me and my listeners, then why couldn't I share my story with others as well?

Being picked up by Auscast Network so early in my podcasting journey was such a wonderful stroke of good fortune. Andy and Liam are accomplished and talented broadcasters and have provided me with support and opportunities I never would have had if we had not connected on social media. My audience has grown with their help and support, and I am honoured to be a part of Auscast Network, Australia's coolest podcast network!

I first met Jules on one of the many podcasting enthusiasts' pages littered across social media. From the outset, I could tell that she was driven. We helped promote her small but growing podcast 'Hong Kong Confidential' on our network. Jules's storytelling, too, has great depth; it can be funny but also dark in places. Her podcast is a unique offering.
– Liam Carter

As one of my podcast guests, Rebecca, said to me, 'you have to go through the heart of what is painful to find a deep and unshakable peace.' I must say that writing this book has allowed me to do that. I have put it all on the table, and it has been a cathartic healing process. I have had many realisations and epiphanies that I did not expect. I have gained a greater understanding of myself and the ways in which I can evolve and improve, but most of all, I have been able to forgive myself, and that is a very powerful feeling.

My Epiphany

Living consciously involves being genuine; it involves listening and responding to others honestly and openly; it involves being in the moment.
– Sidney Poitier

I feel like I have transformed. I am no longer an internet dating neophyte: in fact, I have scaled down my search for love considerably, and now accept that if I am alone forever, then that's okay—I am fulfilled. I have found my tribe in the podcasting world, and that has been a magical journey. I am working on turning any setbacks into successes on my path to finding peace and happiness. I have learned to accept being alone and to turn my focus to feeding my creativity by podcasting, painting, and writing. If I do find someone to share my life with and to love, then that would be wonderful, but it is not my main goal in life now. I have released that pressure and don't feel like a failure or so unlovable anymore because I am single. It's okay just to be me.

Every challenge we face holds the opportunity within it to become better than we are if we consciously look for it. I believe that throughout my life I have used my challenges to become bolder, smarter, and wiser. I can run and hide from my mistakes, or I can face them and learn from them. I have tried to do the latter, but only recently have I truly faced my mistakes head-on by writing this book, and I learned more about myself with every new chapter.

Writing this book has helped me go deeper and really reflect on my personality traits and forgive my flaws. Some of them have been a hard pill to swallow. I need to stop buying affection from others. I have to tune in to my inner self and learn to trust my intuition; not only trust it, but recognise and act on it, not brush it aside. I need to think like a woman, not a teenager when it comes to love and try to approach relationships in a mature and measured manner, not in an idealistic and impractical way.

Interestingly, forgiving myself has been much harder than forgiving Truman, because I blame myself for my choices, not him. Forgiveness sets you free, and writing this book has been a huge step for me in this process. It's so important to find self-compassion and forgiveness; I am very good at doing all of this for others, but not myself. Beyond my online dating mistakes, I need to forgive myself for staying in two abusive relationships and for the mistakes I made as a young parent. I did the best that I could with the tools I had at the time, but if I could go back, I would make some changes to how I parented. I know I did many things right with my choices as a mother, because my daughter is an amazing young woman, of whom I could not be more proud of. She is my greatest joy in life.

I am trying to have an authentic relationship with my past and take a new stance regarding the choices that I made. That would be a position of understanding and self-love rather than of condemnation and shame. This is a work in progress and not always easy, but I am learning to curb self-judgement and be curious and accepting instead. I have had some meaningful life lessons handed to me over the years. I cannot undo what has happened, but I can choose how I respond to these experiences. I can take these lessons one step further to try helping and inspiring others.

I feel like I have achieved something positive by sharing my story. I am very aware that by sharing I may face judgement and, in some cases, ridicule. Of course I worry about negativity and judgement from others, but I am hopeful that the positive responses will outweigh anything negative. It is hard to be vulnerable and put myself out there, but if I can help someone else by sharing my story then that is a wonderful accomplishment. Sometimes we need to see our experiences mirrored back to us in others in order to really know ourselves.

Unfortunately, online dating is also a unique opportunity for scammers to prey on people who are looking for understanding and a connection, and this type of fraud is becoming more and more common. Please be kind to those of us who have been ensnared in this trap, as we are just ordinary people from all walks of life and social classes who have been taken advantage of by consummate professionals who are master manipulators and very skilled at what they do.

Scammers are sneaky, insidious, find vulnerabilities and play on them. It's easy to see in many scammers' approaches and even in relationships characterised by domestic violence that things often operate in a cycle of romance, tension, lashing out, reconciliation, and then back to romance. This way they are able to maintain coercive control and is part of the reason why it is so difficult to get out of these situations. The victim mentality is self-recrimination, blame, shame, and then normalising. I had to break this cycle, and I want to help break it for others. We lose part of ourselves when we have been a victim, and self-care is the antidote.

I had not done my due diligence by investigating Truman before I met him. This would have been a very wise thing to do, but back then, I was not aware of internet dating scams and felt like I had found someone genuine. It was a hard lesson to learn. There are several things you can do to keep safe before you start a relationship with someone online, common red flags you can look for, and types of scams to be aware of that I cover at the end of this book. 'Fool me once, shame on you; fool me twice, shame on me.' Hopefully my story will help destigmatise dating scams and allow others to let go of their shame and guilt, as I am trying to do.

My goal in sharing this story is to encourage people dealing with abuse and manipulation to refocus their life, create an empowering approach, and become successful, confident and happy by seeking support and developing self-love and empathy. Brené Brown talks about comparative suffering and how we often rank our suffering and think that compassion is finite; it is not. Boundless compassion for ourselves and others, along with mutual empathy, is the way forward. I hope those who read my story can see that I could not only survive but also thrive and live life to the fullest. It is wonderful to be exploring what is possible now in my life. If we look for the right support and believe in the possibility of growth, we can do extraordinary things. I hope to bring a perspective to my reader that inspires building resilience and hope by re-evaluating how we deal with our negative experiences. We can free ourselves through forgiveness and become better at dealing with adversity by joining personal development programs. Find something that is right for you. Life coaching and being creative worked for me!

The act of refocusing and reframing my life over the past eight years took the power away from Truman and gave it back to me. Authentically sharing my story will help me to further recover; to do this, I have to claim it and own it—and so can you.

Knowledge is Power

Self-Care

Self-care is critical to becoming mindful and living consciously, making us stronger, more resilient and less susceptible to any person who means us harm. I have included some activities that helped me to work toward this place of well-being below. I plan to continue to do them regularly and make most of them in my life.

These are reliable activities to help develop my best self-care:

- Painting
- Podcasting
- Pilates
- Listening to music
- Receiving a massage
- Meditation
- Breathing awareness
- Journaling
- Swimming
- Singing and dancing
- Eating well
- Sleeping well
- Drinking plenty of water
- Laughing with friends

A Typical Dating Scam Email

Here is one of many scam emails I have received over the years. I reproduced it here just as it came to me, so you can view it as I did.

Hi dear friend,

How are you doing over there? It's nice to come across your profile here and wish we can get to know each other better and see what the future might bring for us. Your profile looks good and I like what I saw. Well, am quite a new member here, a friend of mine who met his soul mate here in the site got me introduced hence I saw your profile and decided to communicate with you. I therefore pray that God may guide us on each and every step we are making in communicating with each other. My name is Braindy Holmes. I was born and brought up in Netherlands But I live and work here in London, I created this account when I went to Australia to visit a friend but now am in London. I am a romantic, energetic and fun loving guy. Please I would like to know you more friends. Distance won't be a barrier if we can trust each other. As we proceed in communication can come over to visit you there in your country or have you invite here in London as I prefer one on one conversation, I am serious and not here to play games. Tell me more about you. And hope to hear from you when time permits you. I seldom online here, so you may drop me your email address or you can reply to me at (braindyholmes a t y h dot come) to enable us to keep in touch. Looking forward to hearing from you.

Remain blessed,
Cheers.
Braindy

There are so many red flags in this email. Firstly, who is named Braindy? I even searched his name on the internet, and nothing came up. It appears that there is not one Braindy in the world. That's a very good clue that the email is bogus.

He begins with 'dear friend'; that kind of formal greeting is also a sign, plus the talk of God. I am not Christian, but I doubt someone who was religious would be talking about God in their first email unless they were on a Christian dating site.

He then goes on to talk about being born in the Netherlands, visiting Australia, and living in London. This is typical of someone who plans to be moving about when you try to meet up. Also, other formal phrases like 'when time permits you' and 'seldom online', in stark contrast to the multiple mistakes in punctuation, spelling, and sentence structure, are a clue this is a potential dating scam.

The mention of his friend finding a soul mate, distance not being a barrier, and that he is not here to play games are all phrases to pull you in to a web of lies. This is just one example of a scam email, and it has some of the clear signs that he is interested in your money, not you.

Red Flags

I was essentially 'catfished' by a career criminal with a rap sheet as long as your arm. Catfish is a term referring to someone pretending to be someone else, using social media or a false online identity to pursue deceptive online romances. This is sort of what happened to me, except Truman used his real photos. Everything else was a lie. Also, many people do not actually meet their catfish—but I did.

MTV's Nev Schulman made the documentary Catfish based on his experiences with an online dating scam in 2010, the same year this happened to me. In the documentary, the term 'catfish' was created when Schulman talked to a fisherman whose wife (Schulman's 'catfish') was scamming Schulman online. The fisherman explains that catfish were added to vats of cod to keep the living fish nimble (and tasty) in transit. 'I thank God for the catfish because we would be droll, boring, and dull if we didn't have somebody nipping at our fin,' he said. That is one way to put a positive spin on it.

These are some of the things that I believe that any person internet dating should look for when trying to ascertain whether the person they are interacting with is real... or a catfish.

Be wary if the person...

- Uses generic statements in their profile without any real information.
- Only has one profile photo.
- Has incredibly attractive profile photos that look like they were taken by a professional.
- Has profile photos that look like they were taken in the country different from the one they say they're living in.
- Calls you 'Dear'.
- Says they're widowed, with or without a child.
- Says their partner has died recently from cancer.
- Uses two first names.
- Has an accent that does not fit with the background or culture they claim to be from.
- Gives you a phone number from a different country than you expected.
- Tells you they are just about to travel overseas, so they cannot meet you straight away.
- Was in your country, left, and is planning to move back in the next few months.
- Writes with poor sentence structure and grammar.
- Uses the word 'God-fearing' or other excessively religious phrasing.
- Says they cannot access popular video chat applications.
- Does not have many social media friends, or their friends are all of the opposite sex.
- Does not share their social media details with you.
- Tells you they love you or that you are their soul mate before they have even met you (this is known as 'love bombing').
- Experiences an unexpected emergency or hardship where they need money.
- Tells you they are thinking of moving to your country or area.

- Refuses to speak on the phone.
- Refuses to send photos other than those on the internet dating page or app.
- Changes any part of their story or details as you get to know them.
- Tells you a sob story about their difficult life to try building an emotional connection with you.
- Claim to have all the same hobbies and interests that you do.
- Wants to save children or build orphanages.
- Sends you photos of themselves dressed to fit a certain lucrative profession.
- Talks about marriage before meeting you.
- Makes excuses not to meet with you (one of the most common is leaving town for work).
- Works in an isolated location that makes it difficult for you to meet them in person.
- Contradicts their own story.
- Gets angry or makes you feel guilty if you question their story or intentions.
- Requests access to your credit card information for any reason.
- Tells you they are rarely on the dating site you met on and asks you to leave the site to communicate by email or a chat service.

Furthermore, use caution if the person…

- Is significantly younger.
- Sends pictures that indicate they are really wealthy, such as standing next to expensive cars, yachts, or fancy houses.
- Talks about living a lavish lifestyle and flaunts their wealth in communication with you, even telling you how much they earn.
- Responds to you very quickly with a long generic statement about looking for love (this indicates that they have just cut and pasted a prepared statement).
- Accidentally sends the same message twice.
- Gets your name wrong.
- Avoids answering questions because the emails they send are often pre-written and generic or are coming from a bot (a computer program that responds to you automatically and tries to get you to click on malicious sites or give your credit card details).
- Uses flowery and dramatic speech and flattery to express love.
- Asks to borrow money and promises to pay you back.
- Requests that you to send money through Western Union.
- Asks you to ship packages to another country.
- Makes unrealistic promises.
- Asks you to cash cheques for them.

Investigate

If someone doesn't raise any of these red flags and appears genuine, you should still do a little research before seriously considering an online relationship.

According to many different online articles, one third of marriages in the USA begin with online dating. It is a very common and often successful way to meet people in this day and age, when everyone is so busy and technology is at our fingertips.

How does the way you represent yourself online affect your safety? When you meet someone online, how can you find out if they are who they really say they are?

Here are some tips that I have learned over the years as a long-term internet dater:

- Do not lie in your own profile.
- Use pictures that are recent.
- Never give them your last name, address, financial information, or the name of your workplace.
- Make sure you get their full name and run an internet search on them.
- Search for them on social media and check out their profiles. (If there is not much action on their page or they have very few friends, this is not a good sign. If they have a large number of friends and they are all the same sex, that is not a good sign, either.)

- Put all of the images they give you into a reverse online image search and see what comes up. If they turn up in other places with different names or you can't find them, then they are likely to be a catfish.

- If you are in the USA, you can search for them on a number of personal information search engines and obtain details such as their address, phone numbers, and family members' names.

- Run an internet search on their place of employment and see if you can find them on employee lists.

- Use a search service that allows you to search the Web for image content and don't forget to try professional networking sites. Not everyone will appear on these sites, but it's worth a look.

- Search for them on dating scammers websites. Maybe they will come up on warning lists.

- Check the distance they are from you if you meet them on a location-based dating mobile app.

- Don't click on links they send you, as these links can lead to malicious sites that can put malware and viruses on your computer.

- Use an account that generates a separate phone number that will redirect calls to your phone so they don't have your actual number.

- Ensure you speak to them face to face via video chat before meeting them. Pay attention to their surroundings.

Meeting Someone

If you decide to meet someone you met online, here are some tips for keeping safe:

- Plan to meet in a busy public place. Never meet someone at their house or in a remote area.
- Tell a friend or two where you are going and when. Ask them to text or call you during the date, firstly to check on you but also to give you an excuse to leave if you want.
- Give your friend every detail you have about the person you're meeting, including their full name, email address, and phone number.
- Never go to another country to meet someone. If you want to meet them, they must come to you.
- Never let them pick you up from your house. Meet them in a neutral public place that is busy.
- Meet for the first time during the day.
- Start with a coffee or a drink. That way if you're not comfortable, you can leave easily.
- If you're not comfortable, politely tell them you're not feeling a connection and say you have to leave.
- Make sure you travel home safely and do not walk off alone into the night. Get a taxi or have someone pick you up.
- DO NOT leave your food or drink unattended. Watch as your drink is poured and handed to you.

- If you are a teenager, you must tell your parents what you're doing. Have one parent or an older sibling go with you on the first date. Any decent person would understand this.
- If you are an adult, there is no reason why you could not take a couple of friends with you for the first date. There is safety in numbers.
- Never go home with them on the first night. It can take some time to get to know someone, and you cannot tell a rapist or a criminal on a first date. Scammers are professional charmers and can fool you easily as they do this for a living.
- Do not get inebriated on a first date. You will become much more vulnerable and less able to make rational decisions.
- Set your smartphone to share your location with friends and family. There are many apps that can assist with this.
- Carry as little cash as possible and do not wear your most expensive jewellery.
- Never lend anyone any money or give them your credit card details.
- Have an exit strategy ready.
- Do not get in a car with your date.
- Set a safe zone with friends or family drinking or dining nearby in case you need them.
- Watch how your date interacts with the public and service staff. This can tell you a lot about their personality.
- Carry pepper spray or a rape whistle.
- Take a personal safety course. There are loads of great videos on video-sharing websites that can help you.
- Be cautious and use good judgement. Trust your instincts.
- Watch out for any red flags and do not ignore them.

In an Emergency

If you ever find yourself in a sticky situation or an emergency like I did, there are things you can do to increase your chances of getting away unharmed, or at the very least, alive.

- Stay calm. Getting angry or hysterical will not help you. The best thing you can do is keep your cool, try your best to think clearly, and keep your wits about you.
- If you can, leave immediately and do not walk home.
- Try to move to an area with other people if things are going wrong.
- Be prepared to leave your belongings if it means getting away safely.
- Use apps that can alert friends or authorities if you are in danger.
- There are apps that can alert others about a dangerous date or someone who has been harassing you.
- Use pepper spray or a rape whistle.
- Scream 'FIRE!' as research shows that people are more likely to come and help you.
- Locate the exits and be ready to run if you can.
- Excuse yourself to go to the toilet and slip out the back door.
- Ask the service staff or a bartender for help.
- Know your own country's emergency number and use it if need be.

Last Words

I wish that I had read a book like this and seen these tips before I started internet dating. These lists are not extensive, but they represent the sum total of my knowledge accumulated over many years of internet dating. I was too open, and perhaps I also felt a little bit invincible. My daughter would say that I was too trusting, I wanted to see the best in everyone, and I expected people to respond and behave the way that I would. Unfortunately, life is not like that, and I had to go through a number of tricky situations before I truly got the message.

I can say that over the last eight years, since my ordeal with Truman, I have pretty much followed my own advice and stayed safe. I have never again planned to meet someone outside of Hong Kong without meeting them in Hong Kong first. I always talk to potential dates on the phone and Skype before meeting up. I have expanded my preferences and am much more open to dating anyone that I click with and am much less fixated on finding someone who resembles my childhood crush, Sidney Poitier—although they do still need to be taller than me! I realise that I need to focus more on the values of the person I am looking for, not their physical characteristics.

I am still single and still perusing dating apps every now and again. Ever the optimist, I have not given up hope of finding love; however, if it doesn't happen, that's fine. Moving to Hong Kong was wonderful for my career, for my ability to earn money, and to provide opportunities for my daughter, but it was not a great move for me to find love and a partner. C'est la vie!

Thanks to one of my 'Hong Kong Confidential' podcast guests, Rebecca, and her podcast 'Own Your Story', I have worked through so much by listening to her and writing this book; this whole journey has changed me for the better. I have seen that I create my own story and have let go of my self-limiting beliefs. I am a good person with integrity; I am compassionate, kind, and passionate about all that I undertake. I am too old and wise to be scammed or mistreated by anyone again. I have the ability to see the good in others, but I will also trust my instincts. I love my life, and I look forward to an exciting future.

END

The truth is: Belonging starts with self-acceptance. Your level of belonging, in fact, can never be greater than your level of self-acceptance, because believing that you're enough is what gives you the courage to be authentic, vulnerable, and imperfect.
–Brené Brown

Jules Hannaford Biography

Jules grew up in rural South Australia before moving to Adelaide, the state capital, and beginning her career as a teacher. She now lives in Hong Kong, the setting of her first book, 'Fool Me Twice', which details the pitfalls and abuse she experienced in her online search for love.

Jules began writing her book in 2010, when she was involved in an internet dating scam. She decided this was an important story to share with other women to prevent them from becoming caught in the same trap and help them make safer, smarter decisions when dating online. It took a long time for her to muster the courage to share her story after battling the shame of choices that landed her in a dangerous situation she counts herself lucky to have survived.

Jules has always had a passion for people and their stories, so she started her podcast 'Hong Kong Confidential' in 2017 to provide a platform for sharing the stories of interesting and unique people in Hong Kong. Just as she knows the importance of sharing their stories on her podcast, she feels that her story can make an important contribution to the safety of those navigating the complicated—and sometimes illusionary—internet dating world.